AF800691

ESTATE PLANNING
FOR SNOWBIRDS

Daniel R. Bernard, Esq.

Jacobs & Whitehall
73-03 Bell Blvd, #10
Oakland Gardens, NY 11364
(888) 570-7338
www.jacobsandwhitehall.com

Ordering Information:

Quantity sales. Special discounts are available on quantity purchases by corporations, associations, and others. For details, contact the publisher at the address above.

Orders by U.S. trade bookstores and wholesalers. Please contact Jacobs & Whitehall: Tel: (888) 991-2766 or visit www.jacobsandwhitehall.com.

Printed in the United States of America

Published in 2021

ISBN: 978-1-951149-97-0

PREFACE

In July 2017 I found myself in the Tampa Convention Center waiting in line with about 2,000 other law school graduates who were hoping to join the ranks of Florida bar admitted attorneys. However, unlike my 2,000 fellow exam takers that day, I was not a recent law school graduate, and I was already able to hold myself out as a lawyer, having taken and passed both the New York and New Jersey bar exams four years earlier. Some thought I was a glutton for punishment because they could not think of a less fun way to spend two days in Tampa, in July no less. However, there was a method to my madness.

After graduating from Rutgers School of Law-Newark and serving a one-year clerkship with a New Jersey Superior Court judge, I began practicing law as an estate planning attorney. Then to better assist and advise my higher net worth clients with their estate planning and complex estate tax planning I attended New York University School of Law in pursuit of a

Master of Laws (LL.M) in taxation, which I pursued part-time; traveling into Manhattan for night classes and eating a lot of Penn Station pizza on the way home. I completed my LL.M. in the fastest way possible way, part-time, by taking summer classes and the maximum credit load each semester. After completing my LL.M. the next logical step for me was to take the Florida bar exam. The reason I wanted to take the Florida bar exam and gain admission to the Florida bar was to better serve New York's ever growing snowbird population.

Far too often I meet with people through my seminars or referred to me from my other snowbird clients, who simply have no idea about the complexities snowbirding adds to their estates. The good news is, with proper estate planning, specifically geared to snowbirds, these complexities can be easily mitigated. My hope with this book is that you will better understand the complications being a snowbird can add to your estate.

Dedication

For Grace and Benjamin, my reason for planning.

DISCLAIMER

This publication is intended to be used for educational purposes only. No legal advice is being given, and no attorney-client relationship is intended to be created by reading this material. The author assumes no liability for any errors or omissions or for how this book or its contents are used or interpreted, or for any consequences resulting directly or indirectly from the use of this book. For legal or any other advice, please consult an experienced attorney or the appropriate expert, who is aware of the specific facts of your case and is knowledgeable in the law in your jurisdiction.

Twomey Latham, Shea, Kelley,
Dubin & Quartararo, LLP.

33 West Second St.
P.O. Box 9398
Riverhead, NY 11901
(631) 727 2180
www.suffolklaw.com

TABLE OF CONTENTS

About The Author

As a trust and estates attorney, the primary focus of my practice is estate planning, trust and estate administration, estate tax planning, business succession planning, and estate litigation, with an emphasis on estate planning for snowbirds. Having been admitted to practice law in both New York and Florida, I have the unique ability—unlike most attorneys who are licensed in only one state—to represent clients effectively, appear in court, and probate wills, and administer estates in both New York and Florida. I have been quoted in The Wall Street Journal, Newsday, and U.S. News and World Report in articles related to estate planning and taxation issues. I have also been a guest on the "Ask the Attorney" show, the "Dead Celebrity Podcast," and the "Law You Should Know" radio show and podcast to discuss estate planning for snowbirds.

Why Did You Want To Write This Book?

When I meet with snowbird clients and start explaining the special circumstances created by their status as a snowbird, they tend to not only be very surprised by the significant effect being a snowbird has on their estate, but also are very grateful for the information. My hope is that this book will reach many more snowbirds than the 20 to 30 that I can typically help at one of my seminars. A snowbird who has the information contained in this book can save their heirs a lot of time, a significant amount of money, and many headaches.

CHAPTER 1

THE SNOWBIRD MIGRATION BEGINS

Jerry Seinfeld famously quipped, "My parents didn't want to move to Florida, but they turned sixty and that's the law."

Although, this is obviously not an actual statute in New York, for many New Yorkers, as our friends and relatives get older, and retire, it has certainly seemed like it is a law on the books in New York because many of these friends are relatives are all of a sudden nowhere to be found come winter. While we shovel snow and slip on ice, these snowbirds are playing golf, fishing, and walking the beach at night.

If you are a snowbird, you likely carefully planned exactly where in Florida you move for the winter. Maybe like many of New York's snowbirds you chose Florida's east coast, preferring Boca Raton or West Palm Beach. Or maybe you preferred the west coast of Florida, and bought a home in Naples or Fort Myers. Or perhaps you do not want to be as close to the beach and wanted to live that Disney vacation for the whole winter and chose to settle closer to the tourist hot spot Orlando, or a little further north in Florida's ever growing retirement community, The Villages. No matter where you decided to settle, you likely carefully thought it out.

Next, each year as the too short, beautiful fall weather turns to bitter cold, you carefully consider the best time to leave for Florida and the best time to return, especially if you want to be considered a Florida resident, and no longer a New York resident for tax purposes (more on this later).

In my experience, despite all of the careful planning, few snowbirds realize the potential estate hazards the multistate lifestyle can come with. The good news is these hazards can be easily avoided with proper estate planning.

What Can Occur If A Snowbird Hasn't Properly Planned Or Updated Their Estate Planning Documents To Accommodate Their Lifestyle?

Snowbird estate planning issues arise in three tiers. A first-tier issue is when someone is living in or spending significant time Florida, but still only has their New York estate planning documents in place, such as a New York form health care proxy, living will, and durable power of attorney. The issue can arise when one of these documents needs to be used in Florida, because Floridians (and their New York counterparts) are used to seeing their state's form. For example, in Florida rather than a health care proxy, the form for appointing someone to make your health care decisions is called a declaration of health care surrogate. Furthermore, the New York power of attorney form looks a lot different than the Florida one.[1] Florida medical providers are likely unfamiliar with New York estate planning documents and will need their legal department to review your New York form health care proxy before accepting it as valid, as would a Florida bank need their legal department to review a New York durable power of attorney. This could leave the individual and their family members in limbo during a serious medical situation. This first-tier issue is very easily mitigated by having the documents for both states. First tier issues effect all snowbirds.

An example of a second-tier issue that could arise is passing away owning real property (real estate) in multiple states. Under these circumstances, the decedent's heirs will have to probate the estate in every state where the decedent owned real estate. For example, if the decedent owned a house in New York and a condo in Florida, then their heirs would have to

---

[1] Please see appendix starting on page 77 for examples of the form Durable Power of Attorney for New York and the form Durable Power of Attorney for Florida, as an example of the differences between the documents for New York and Florida.

commence a probate in New York and another probate in Florida, even if the condo in Florida is the only property the decedent owned in Florida. This can be a big headache for the heirs, and it's going to cost them a lot of unnecessary time and money. However, this issue can be easily mitigated with proper estate planning specifically for snowbirds. The second tier snowbird issue effects all snowbirds who own their homes in both states.

The third-tier issue branches off into two sectors. The first has to do with the fact that snowbirds can live in multiple states but be a resident of only one state (which is called their "domicile"). This is significant for high-net-worth individuals because New York imposes a myriad of taxes on its residents, including a state level estate tax and a state level income tax, whereas Florida does not impose an estate tax or an income tax on its residents. For snowbirds of more modest wealth, the question might be about the state in which they plan to utilize Medicaid for long-term care expenses. Medicaid is only going to pay for nursing home care for residents of that state. For a snowbird, this third-tier issue boils down to asking the following questions: which state am I actually a resident of right now, and which state do I want to be a resident of? This third tier estate planning issue effects high net worth snowbirds and those snowbirds who are seeking long term care paid for by Medicaid.

What Are Some Of The Most Important Questions You Ask Potential Clients Who Are Snowbirds?

The number one question to ask a snowbird is whether or not they already have an estate plan in place. If they do, then it may be as simple as adding a few documents or incorporating some snowbird planning into the current plan. Regardless of the answer to the first question, the second question would be about their assets. It will be necessary to get a sense of what assets they have and how they own those assets. Have they moved any assets into a trust? Do they own assets in multiple states? What's their net worth? Should we plan for the client to be a Florida resident or a New York resident? These questions can provide a jumping of point to craft their individualized estate plan.

CHAPTER 2

WHAT ARE THE BASIC ITEMS OF AN ESTATE PLAN?

Before I address estate planning issues particular to snowbirds, it is important to address the basic documents that make up an estate plan. There are four key documents to any estate plan, and without them, you simply to not have a complete estate plan. Four key documents make up the complete estate plan: 1. A health care proxy; 2. A living will; 3. A durable power of attorney; and 4. A Last Will and Testament. Many people assume an estate plan is just their Will, but there could be a period of time prior to death where you cannot make your own medical decisions or manage your own financial affairs due to incapacity. That is where these other documents come into place.

The first document is a health care proxy, which appoints someone to make certain health care decisions in the event of incapacity. Only one health care agent can be appointed at a time, and that health care agent is supposed to make the health care decisions that they think the individual would make based on their wishes, if those wishes are known. The reason only one health care agent can be appointed at a time is to avoid the potential of two health care agents arguing over what they believe is the right decision, and creating a deadlock when a critical medical decision is needed quickly. Although you can only appoint one health care agent at a time, you can appoint any number of backup health care agents, and each agent would serve in the order of appointment should your initial health care agent become unavailable, such as by predeceasing you, being unable to act, or choosing not to act as health care agent. In Florida this document is called a Declaration of Health Care Surrogate.

In conjunction with the health care proxy, the living will is an advance directive for end-of-life care. If two doctors agree that the individual has an irreversible condition and there is no chance of recovery, then the living will would allow the health care agent to tell the doctors to make the individual as comfortable as possible and to let them go. The key focus of this document is for compassionate care at end of life. In Florida this document is called a Declaration.

The third document is the durable power of attorney, which appoints someone to make financial decisions. The power of attorney is durable, meaning the person appointed will be able to handle all of the individual's financial affairs should they become incapacitated and unable to do so themselves. This includes handling banking transactions, paying bills, and possibly doing Medicaid planning to get the individual into a nursing home. Unlike the health care proxy, there can be more than one person appointed as power of attorney. If you appoint more than one person, you can also decide whether these individuals have to work together or can work separately. If they have to work together, it creates a system of checks and balances, whereby they would have to canvas on all the checks, go to the bank together, etc. If they are allowed to work separately, then they can divide the duties and there will be less burden on one person. One word of caution, the power of attorney can be used by the person you appoint as soon as it is signed. For this reason my firm keeps the signed power of attorney in our vault for safekeeping and will only release upon your request or upon your demonstrated incapacity. In Florida this document is also called a Durable Power of Attorney. One last note on powers of attorney, these documents are statutory documents in New York and Florida. As such, the statutes, and therefore the form documents can change. For example, Florida updated its power of attorney form in 2017 and New York updated its power of attorney form in 2021. So, it is worthwhile to make sure you have the latest form.

The fourth document is the one we all think about when we think about estate planning, and that's the Last Will and Testament. In a Will, an individual can appoint guardians for their children and an executor who will administer the estate. The creator of the Will dictates how their assets pass and who they will pass to. Trusts can be created within the will so that the assets don't go to someone they shouldn't, such as a child who has financial issues or is not good with money. If the money is going to young grandchildren, and the creator of the will doesn't think they are old enough to have the money, then the money can be placed into a trust until the grandchildren reach a certain age.

CHAPTER 3

ARE MY ESTATE PLANNING DOCUMENTS CREATED IN NEW YORK ENOUGH TO COVER ME?

It is not sufficient for a snowbird to have estate planning documents only in New York or only in Florida, because they need state-specific versions of those documents in each state. My number one recommendation is that snowbirds have a health care proxy, living will, and power of attorney document for New York and for Florida. This will make the snowbird's life much easier down the line when they may need to use those documents in one or the other state.

The second issue that could arise with regard to having estate planning documents only in one state is that those documents might not take into consideration that the individual owns assets in the other state, or spends part of their time in another state. It may be necessary to move Florida property and/or New York property into a trust in order to avoid probate in Florida and/or New York and save heirs the time, expense, and headache of having to deal with two probates. Even if someone thinks they have a great New York estate plan, it would still be a good idea to talk to an estate planning attorney about their new snowbird lifestyle and ensure that the existing estate plan does not need to be updated.

Are A Lot Of People Surprised That Their Estate Planning Documents May Not Carry Over From State To State?

Almost every snowbird client at almost every seminar is very surprised that becoming a snowbird can have such a big impact on their estate. This is something that compelled me to write this book; I want to get this important information to those who need it most, and make everyone's life a little bit easier.

Where Should Someone Keep The Physical Copies Of Their Estate Planning Documents When They Have A Snowbird Lifestyle?

The Florida version of the health care proxy (i.e. the declaration of health care surrogate), living will, and durable power of attorney should be kept in Florida, and the New York versions should be kept in New York. This will make it easy for the individual's agent to access and use them regardless of which state they are in.

Most attorney offices (including mine) will keep their clients' wills in a waterproof, fireproof vault for safekeeping. The purpose of this is not to hold client's documents hostage, but to ensure that their heirs know exactly where to access the Will or other documents should they need them. This also protects against the possibility of the Will being destroyed by accident. Even if the Will is destroyed by accident (or lost), the presumption is that the Will was intentionally destroyed. This means your heirs would need to start an administration proceeding as if there was never an estate plan to begin with. This is a disaster, because number one the time and money you spent putting your estate plan together is wasted, and two your wishes will not be followed. Instead, your estate will pass via the intestacy statute of the state where you were a resident upon your death. This could mean assets passing to people you did not want them to pass to. My office also keeps a copy of any other estate planning documents created by our clients in the vault for safekeeping. The attorney's office is probably the safest place, especially if it's an established firm that isn't going anywhere. People should make sure that their heirs know that the estate planning firm is holding onto the documents for safekeeping.

The worst possible place to keep these important documents is a safe deposit box, because when the individual dies, no one will be able to access that box until someone is appointed as executor or as personal representative, and no one can be appointed as executor or personal representative until the Will is probated. If the Will is in the safe deposit box, then someone in the family, such as the presumed executor or personal representative, will have to go to the surrogate's court, file a motion, and open a proceeding just to access the safe deposit box to find the Will. This adds a lot of unnecessary time and expense to your estate administration.

Will It Cost Me A Fortune To Have Estate Planning Documents Done For Both New York And Florida?

When I prepare documents for my snowbird clients, it really does not cost more than it does to prepare documents for non-snowbird clients. Updating documents for tier-one issues just requires a health care proxy for Florida, a living will, and a durable power of attorney. This is not a process that's going to break the bank. When dealing with tier-two issues, creating a trust for the Florida house in order to avoid Florida probate, is not really not going to cost more than it does for someone who only lives in New York and wants to avoid New York probate. For the tier-three issue of estate tax and long-term care planning, the costs are comparable to the costs for people who only live in New York.

The costs of revising your estate plan for your snowbird lifestyle should be heavily outweighed by the savings to your heirs. Ultimately, one primary goal of all properly drafted estate plans should be the orderly disposition of assets at death. When a snowbird does proper estate planning, their heirs can avoid the time, expense and headaches of probate in multiple states and can ensure their heirs receive their assets in the most time effective and efficient manner possible. Ultimately, avoiding probate with a properly drafted estate plan will essentially pass more assets to your heirs, through the savings in the cost of probate in New York and Florida.

CHAPTER 4

HOW CAN WE SET UP OUR ESTATE PLANNING DOCUMENTS IN BOTH NEW YORK & FLORIDA?

It's not necessary for a person to decide where their final home will be, because things certainly change; it's only possible to make the best plan for the current situation. My recommendation is to speak to an estate planning attorney who is licensed in both New York and Florida so that they can provide the best advice in terms of a solid plan as of 'today.' Then, the plan can be revisited every five years or whenever there is a major life event. Revisiting the plan is important to ensure that it makes sense given the current laws and the individual's situation. For example, the federal and New York State estate tax exemptions have significantly changed a few different times over the last five years. Another reason to revisit your estate planning documents is the fiduciaries you appoint as executor or personal representative, health care agent, and trustee, may make sense today, but be a nightmare in five years. We often forget whom we appoint in these roles, so reviewing every so often is a reminder of who will manage our affairs and a chance to revise if necessary.

Once We Have Estate Planning Documents In Place For Both Florida And New York, How Often Do We Need To Revisit Those Plans?

I recommend that all clients revisit their estate planning documents every five years or any time there is a major life event. Examples of major life events are: divorce, either you or one of your children, deaths of a spouse or child, and significant increases in wealth.

For What Reasons Do People Commonly Need To Update Their Estate Planning Documents?

There are many events which could warrant an update to estate planning documents. For instance, if a person's child encounters financial difficulty, then it might make sense to create a lifetime trust for them rather than leave the assets to them outright.

Another example is the birth of a grandkid to whom the individual wants to leave money.

If the person's spouse or child passes away and that spouse was a primary fiduciary, health care agent, durable power of attorney, and/or personal representative, then it would make sense to update the documents.

Any divorce or remarriage might constitute a discussion about intentions and an adjustment to the estate planning documents. Marriages that occur later in life often involve spouses who each want their assets to go to their children, and this is something that would have to be planned for properly under the law, whether through a prenuptial or postnuptial agreement. Additionally, it is possible to provide for a spouse during their lives through a special trust called a "qualified terminal interest property" trust, wherein the spouse would receive the trust income for life, but at their death the remaining trust assets pass to your heirs. This gives the surviving spouse access to the income from your assets but allows you to ultimately pass that asset to your own heirs (your children or grandchildren). This type of trust could also own your house, giving your spouse lifetime use of the property that you share, but ultimately ensuring the house eventually passes to your heirs.

CHAPTER 5

DIFFERENCE BETWEEN NEW YORK AND FLORIDA ESTATE PLANNING LAWS

One of the main differences between New York and Florida estate planning laws is that in New York, anyone over the age of 18 who is not a convicted felon and is competent to serve can be appointed as executor. In Florida, the role of executor is called personal representative, and it must be someone who is over the age of 18, a US citizen, not a convicted felon, competent to serve, and a Florida resident or someone who is related to the creator of the Will, such as their spouse, sibling, cousin, aunt, or uncle or a spouse of a person related to the creator of the Will. A non-Florida resident and a non-family member cannot serve as personal representative. This can become problematic when the backup personal representative is needed, but was appointed in New York and is a non-Florida resident and a non-family member. Such as when a trusted advisor such as an accountant or financial advisor is appointed as executor. Under such circumstances, a family member or Florida resident would have to step up and serve as personal representative.

Another important difference between the estate planning laws in New York and Florida is that New York, recognizes and enforces what are called in terrorem clauses or no-contest clauses. This is a basic part of every Will and every revocable trust, and it basically says that if anyone contests the Will or trust, then they will not receive whatever distribution of assets they were set to receive. This clause will be used if it is suspected that someone with standing will contest the Will or trust. Persons with standing include spouses, children, and others who would inherit assets in the absence of the Will. This means that a neighbor of the deceased who believed he would receive the deceased's vehicle would have no standing to contest the estate.

In contesting a Will, an individual is essentially saying that the Will should be thrown out because the creator of the Will was not competent to sign the Will or was under undue influence of someone else. The purpose of the contest might be to revive a previous will that was more favorable to them, or moving forward without a Will so that the heirs share in the estate under the state's intestacy laws. If a client wants to disinherit a child or grandchild, we typically would recommend leaving a small bequest to that disinherited person and adding an in terrorem clause so that that person would not receive anything should they try to contest the Will. For example, the client might decide to leave only $10,000 to a son who they haven't spoken to in 20 years. By adding the in terrorem clause, that son would lose the $10,000 inheritance by trying to contest the Will.

In New York, these clauses are 100 percent enforceable, but in Florida, they are not enforceable. If this clause is going to be a part of an estate plan, then it's important to distinguish that the will be probated in New York where it will be enforced. I include the in terrorem clause in every Will and trust that I create for my clients, because no one knows whether their Will or trust will be contested, nor can we predict where your Will or trust will be administered; so, it just makes sense to include the in terrorem clause.

Another major difference between New York and Florida law is that New York imposes an estate tax and Florida does not. The estate tax threshold for New York is very high, at almost six million dollars for 2021. This means no estate tax would be taken out if the assets are under that threshold. For high-net-worth individuals, this can be a significant tax because it's a progressive tax that tops out at 16 percent. On average, people who do have to pay New York estate tax pay about a 13 percent tax on their estate.

New York does not have a gift tax, but any gift that is made within three years of death is brought back into the estate for valuing the estate for estate tax purposes. This is to avoid deathbed gifts, where people just give away all of their assets right before they pass away and thereby avoid the New York estate tax completely.

Florida does not have an estate tax nor a gift tax. This means Florida allows people to do unlimited tax free gifting prior to death and not have any state-level estate tax imposed for those gifts at death; again, this would not be the case in New York if the person did not survive beyond three years of the gifting.

CHAPTER 6

DIFFERENCE BETWEEN NEW YORK LAW AND FLORIDA LAW IN PROBATE MATTERS

In every Florida county, e-filing is accepted. This means that we can probate Florida estates from New York by filing everything online. As long as the personal representative is a family member, they can administer the entire estate from New York. I've administered multiple estates where the personal representative never had to set foot in Florida. In New York, only some counties allow for e-filing.

In Florida, a notice of publication must be made for the estate in order to notice creditors. This publication usually comes in around $750. In New York, this isn't necessary unless the surrogate's court tells us that we have to publish a notice to either creditors or to an heir that we can't find. In both places, the surrogate's court is going to dictate how the executor or personal representative can manage the estate. They can also put restrictions on the personal representative. For example, they may be able to collect assets only up to a certain amount without a court order, and then publishing additional notices could be made mandatory. They may need to appoint a guardian ad litem for heirs that cannot be located. New York and Florida can do that, but New York seems to be more aggressive with it.

How Do We Avoid Probate, And Why Should That Be One Of The Primary Goals?

Probate is time-consuming and expensive, but easily avoidable. Avoiding probate will save heirs money in legal fees, publication fees, and court fees to the surrogate's court. It's also going to save them a lot of time because they won't have to get involved with time-consuming court processes. When a document is filed with the Surrogate's court, it could take weeks to get any response and for the court to appoint a personal representative who can manage the estate. Florida courts seem to move faster than New York courts, but avoiding probate in both states is still the best course of action.

Probate can be avoided by transferring assets into a trust. There are many different kinds of trusts, but if the goal is to simply avoid probate and nothing else, then the best type would be a revocable trust. As the name suggests, this type of trust is revocable, which means it can be changed at any time, and adding or removing assets is not a taxable event. The trust is basically just another way for the individual to hold assets; the assets are still owned by the individual, and the individual would still be eligible to receive tax exemptions on any property owned in the trust (e.g. a homestead exemption in Florida, a STAR exemption in New York). The only difference is that a any asset placed in the trust would have the name of the revocable trust rather than the name of the individual. So if you transfer your house(s) to the trust, the deed and property tax bills would include the words "revocable trust." If even one probate asset is left out of the trust, probate would need to be done for that one asset. For this reason, it's very important to make sure that all probate assets are put into the trust. Probate assets are all assets that do not have a named beneficiary, such as houses, LLCs, corporations, and other business assets. Life insurance, brokerage accounts and IRAs do not need to be transferred to the revocable trust, since those assts have beneficiary designations.

The major benefit is that any assets that are in the revocable trust will bypass probate. Upon the individual's passing, the trustee would manage the trust assets and distribute them as per the terms of the trust. In other words, instead of the personal representative having to go to probate court and becoming appointed as executor or the personal representative, they would simply accept their appointment as trustee and could immediately begin acting as trustee. This means that they could list the house for sale, remove cash from a brokerage account or bank account to pay estate expenses, if the trust was the owner or beneficiary of the account, and distribute the assets as per the terms of the trust without the surrogate court's overview.

This doesn't mean that they could run roughshod over the other heirs, because they would still have to account for what they did to manage the trust; if they are not doing things properly, then the other beneficiaries could get the court involved and force the trustee to follow the terms of the trust. The trustee could also be charged back if they're not managing the trust properly. Meaning they would have to reimburse the trust for any assets they misappropriated. That being said, an individual should appoint a trustee who they do not believe will mismanage the estate.

One way to think about the revocable trust is that it essentially serves as a modern version of a Will. You would still have a Will, but it would be a simple Will called a "pour over" Will that simply says to transfer all of your probate assets into your revocable trust. The Will essentially serves as a safety net, in the event any probate assets are missed. Your revocable trust is a substitute for a traditional Will because it essentially tells us what happens to your assets when you pass away, can create sub-trusts within the revocable trust, such as lifetime trusts for your children or trusts for your grandchildren, who may be too young to inherit and have free reign over the inheritance, and the revocable trust will appoint a trustee to administer the trust. The trustees job is similar to an executor, in that the trustee will follow the terms of your trust and distribute your assets based on those terms.

What Is Ancillary Probate And How Can It Be Avoided?

An ancillary probate is a probate in addition to the primary probate. The primary probate will be in the state where the individual is a resident, and the ancillary probate will be in any other state where the individual owns real estate. For example, if someone lives in New York, has a business in New York, and has most of their assets in New York, then their primary probate is going to be in New York. If they have a condo in Florida, then there would have to be an ancillary probate just for that Florida condo. Although the term "ancillary" makes it seem like it is not very difficult, an ancillary probate—even if it's only for one asset—and a full probate require the exact same amount of time, effort, and expense.

An ancillary probate is very easily avoidable by creating a revocable or irrevocable trust, and by putting the asset that's in another state (most likely Florida) into that trust. If the trust controls it and we don't have to do a probate in that state, then the trustee can distribute the asset based on the terms of the trust.

The simple fact is that with proper estate planning a snowbird should not need to have their estate probated. Avoiding probate will save that snowbird's estate a lot of time, money, effort and headaches.

CHAPTER 7

HOW TO DETERMINE WHICH STATE TO CONSIDER OUR LEGAL DOMICILE?

No one knows the exact number of people who split their time between New York and Florida each year. However, Florida reported that between September 2020 and March 2021, over 33,000 New Yorkers exchanged their New York driver's license for a Florida driver's license.[2] Florida has also reported that between April 2019 and April 2021 a total of 104,960 New Yorkers exchanged their New York driver's license for a Florida driver's license.[3] Additionally, data from state auditing indicates that well over 3,000 new high-net-worth individuals start to head to Florida from New York each year and join the ranks of the "snowbirds".[4]

When deciding which state to consider the legal domicile, the primary consideration is about taxes. The estate tax in New York is up to 16 percent of the estate assets, but there is no estate tax in Florida. Florida does

---

[2] See Skelding, Conor. "The Sixth Borough: Florida State Records Quantify Defections from NY." *New York Post*, New York Post, 15 May 2021, nypost.com/2021/05/15/florida-records-quantify-number-of-defections-from-ny/.

[3] See Id.

[4] See Frank, Robert. "Tax Collectors Chase Rich New Yorkers Moving to Low-Tax States. Auditors Inspect Cell Records, Even Your Dog's Vet Bills." CNBC, CNBC, 8 Mar. 2019, www.cnbc.com/2019/03/08/tax-collectors-chase-rich-new-yorkers-moving-to-low-tax-states.html.

not have a gift tax, whereas New York will include gifts made within three years of the death in the taxable estate.

Florida does not have a state-level income tax, and that includes the capital gains tax. The federal capital gains get a preferred rate of between 0 and 20 percent based on income, but New York does not do that. New York taxes capital gains in the same way as ordinary income, so it's taxed between four percent and 8.82 percent. Typically in retirement people will start to recognize capital gains as they sell assets that they have accumulated for their retirement, such as taxable brokerage accounts and investment properties. A New York resident will pay a state level income tax on those gains, whereas a Florida resident will not. Unfortunately, federal income tax is required no matter where in the US someone lives.

It should be noted that while both Florida and New York accept anyone as a resident, New York is particularly aggressive with conducting residency audits on people who claim to no longer be residents of New York State. If someone leaves New York with no intention of coming back to New York, that's easy to prove, but that's not the case with snowbirds. Snowbirds typically want to leave New York for the really cold winter months and come back for a milder summer than the summer Florida offers. When a snowbird claims that Florida is their domicile and they only return to New York for visits, New York is very aggressive in insisting that the snowbird is actually a resident of New York, so that they will be subject to New York tax.

The secondary consideration when deciding which state to consider your legal domicile has to do with Medicaid planning for nursing home care. If an individual plans on using Medicaid to pay for nursing home care in New York, then they will need to be a resident of New York; the same is true for Florida. In both New York and Florida, a person can qualify for Medicaid relatively quickly. The issue is preserving assets prior to making a Medicaid application.

What Points Of Evidence Will New York And Florida Consider In Determining The Legal Domicile?

New York is very aggressive in the residency audits. In recent years, they have been doing about

3,000 per year, which might not seem like a lot, but within the last ten years, they have collected about a billion dollars in tax revenue through these residency audits. On average, they collect about $140,000 per residency audit in unpaid New York State taxes. So, New York is very aggressive on this because it's very lucrative for them.

The burden of proving non-resident status is on the individual, not the state of New York. There are two different ways that New York will attempt to say that someone is still a New York resident. The first way is by stating you are still domiciled. In other words, they will say that since the person is domiciled in New York, they are a resident of New York. The term 'domicile' is really a legal term of art, because a person can be a resident of multiple states, but can really only have one domicile, which is their home (not their 'house'). It is the place where the individual always intends to return to. New York will tell snowbirds that they vacation in Florida each year, but always intend to return to New York, so New York is where they are domiciled.

In proving that New York is an individual's domicile, the state is going to look at five factors, the first of which is the house. If someone lives in a very large, very expensive house in New York and has a two-bedroom condo in Florida, they are going to challenge the assertion that the large house that they have had for decades and/or where they raised their family is their vacation house. They will compare the New York property and the Florida property to see if they're equal in terms of value.

Active business involvement is the second factor they will consider. For instance, if someone claims to live in Florida and be a resident of Florida but actively manages their business in New York, then New York is going to point to their level of involvement in the New York business in arguing that they are a resident of New York.

The third factor is the amount of time spent in New York versus Florida. Usually, the argument is that if the person spent most of their time in New York, then they are a New York resident.

The fourth factor is the location of items "near and dear" to the individual, which is sometimes referred to as the Teddy Bear Rule. For instance, the individual may be asked where they keep their wedding album, family photos, stamp collection, and other items of particular value to them. The argument being that you generally keep your most important items in your home, not your vacation property.

The fifth and final factor is family connections, meaning where the individual's family members live. If someone claims to be a Florida resident but their spouse and minor children live in New York, then they are going to say that they are a resident of New York.

No one factor is determinative. New York will weigh all of the factors to assert that you are still a New York State resident.

Even if you can prove that you have changed your domicile to Florida, New York will apply the 183-day rule to claim that someone who is not domiciled in New York is a resident of New York nonetheless. This is called being a statutory resident. The rule is that if the individual has a permanent place of abode in New York, which means a house, or even a room in someone else's house. It is not necessary for the individual to own the property in order for it to be considered a place of abode in New York, and if the individual spends in the aggregate more than 183 days of the taxable year in New York, then they will be considered a New York resident.

In order for a person to prove that they spent fewer than 183 days in New York, they must literally count each day of the year and prove where they were located. The auditors have been known to pull phone records to see where people were placing calls each day. They have also been known to subpoena credit card receipts to see where people were purchasing things each day.

It has been held that if a person keeps a contemporaneous calendar, which is a calendar that they use every single day to write which state they are in, as opposed to going back in time and filling in the calendar once they are being audited, then the calendar will be considered proof of their location on each day.

Another piece of advice would be to buy a newspaper with a credit card and keep the receipt as evidence of where the individual was located. Lastly, there are a variety of cell phone applications that can be downloaded to your phone and that will through geo-tracking show where you were each day. These apps have been accepted as proof of which state a person is in during audit.

When someone is audited, it's always going to come down to a battle of the evidence. The burden is on the taxpayers to show proof that they are not domiciled in New York and spent less than 183 days in New York. The number one way for a person to show that they are not domiciled in New York is to show that their house in Florida is comparable or nicer than the house in New York.

When it comes to active business involvement, it's important that the individual scale down their business involvement in New York. It is possible to move ones business to Florida in a tax free reorganization. The Florida business would retain the same tax identification number, and attributes. If you intend to continue to run your business from Florida, and if it is possible to move the business to Florida, then this may be a prudent step to avoid the active business involvement factor.

It's also important that they are cognizant of how much time they spend in New York and mindful of the 183-day rule. However, there is no hard and fast rule for time spent in New York for domicile. You could spend two weeks in New York, but not spend more than one week anywhere else throughout the year and be considered a New York resident.

To deal with the factor of items near and dear, the individual could just move those items to Florida and prove that they did so in one of two ways: by making a recording showing those items in the Florida location, or by hiring a moving company to move the items to Florida, and getting a copy of the signed inventory sheet.

Lastly, in terms of family connections, the focus will be on where the spouse lives, and where younger children (rather than adult children or grandchildren) live. If someone's spouse and young children live in

New York yet they claim to be a resident of Florida, that's going to be a tough sell. Family connections is however the least used factor to prove domicile. The house, business involvement and items near and dear are much more likely to be weighed against you.

There are some other steps that a person can take in order to show that they are not a resident of New York. One step is to file a Florida declaration of domicile in the office of the clerk of the circuit court of the Florida County where the individual lives.[5] Please note, filing a declaration of domicile is different than applying for the homestead exemption. If you want the homestead exemption on your Florida property you must make a separate application.

Another step would be to file an application for a homestead exemption for the Florida residence so that they use Florida property tax exemptions instead of New York property tax exemptions. You must be a

---

[5] Please see appendix starting on page 122 for the form Declaration of Domicile for Florida's top snowbird counties.

Florida resident for one year before you qualify for the homestead exemption. If you are receiving the STAR discount in New York you are not eligible for the homestead exemption and vice versa. If you begin to receive the Florida homestead exemption, you will lose your New York STAR discount.

It would also be helpful to exchange your New York driver's license for a Florida driver's license, register your vehicles in Florida, and register to vote in Florida. In addition, you should begin banking with a bank located in Florida as opposed to New York.

If you are a part of a church or place of worship in New York, or a member of clubs within New York, you should join similar organizations in Florida.

You should also update your estate planning documents to include the Florida documents, such as the health care surrogate, Florida declaration, and Florida durable power of attorney, and consider the efficacy of their will and any trusts based on Florida law so that you can show the auditors that you updated your estate plan to reflect that you are a Florida resident.

CHAPTER 8

WHY IS DETERMINING THE DOMICILE IMPORTANT FOR HIGH-NET-WORTH ESTATES?

In Florida, there is no state-level estate tax, but there is in New York. If an individual has a $6 million or greater estate in New York or a couple has a $12 million estate or greater, then they could be subject to millions of dollars in estate tax, whereas in Florida, the person's heirs would not have to pay any state-level estate tax. It is important to note that New York State, as does the federal government, allows for an unlimited marital deduction. Meaning a spouse can transfer an unlimited amount of money at death to their surviving spouse. The estate tax would be collected on the whole estate of the second spouse to die.

For example, with proper planning, a husband and wife can currently transfer approximately $12 million of property without incurring any New York estate tax. However, take that same couple and add $3 million to their net worth ($15 million net worth) and, an estate tax of approximately, $950,000 would be due to New York State upon the second spouse's death. That same couple if they were Florida residents would avoid paying any state level estate tax.

As far as gifting during life, New York State and Florida both do not impose a gift tax. However, New York State will "claw back" the value of any gifts made within three years of death. So, if a person makes $1 million in gifts and then dies two years later with a $5 million estate, New York will claw back the $1 million of gifts and value the estate at $6 million, subjecting the estate to estate tax.

The federal government applies a unified estate and gift tax, meaning you have a certain level of exemption to use either during life via gifting or at death via the estate tax exemption. When gifts are made a gift tax return should be filed so the government can keep track of the amount of estate and gift tax credit you have used during life. However, each year, an individual and their spouse can each make gifts of up to $15,000 per person per year that do not count towards their lifetime estate and gift tax credit. These gifts are called "annual exclusion gifts." For example, a husband and wife could together gift $30,000 per year to any number of people. For higher net-worth individuals, $30,000 might not sound like a lot. However, if someone has three kids and seven grandkids and they make these gifts to a trust for their benefit, then over a 10-year period that would amount to three million dollars. For snowbird planning purposes, the key to annual exclusion gifts are that they are not subject to the New York State gift claw back.

New York Tax Law imposes New York State personal income tax on "resident individuals." Again, pursuant to New York Tax Law a resident individual is defined as person domiciled within the state or a person maintains a house in New York and spends in the aggregate more than 183 days of the year in New York. Further, New York residents are taxed on all their income both inside and outside of New York State. In contrast, Florida does not have a state income tax.

How Should Real Estate Owned In Each State Be Handled When It Comes To Avoiding Probate?

Real estate that is owned by a snowbird should be held by a trust, because if they own the real estate outright, then they could end up having to do a probate in one or both states. This is based on the constitutional doctrine of sovereignty between the states, meaning no court in one state may determine ownership of real estate in another state. In other words, a New York court cannot determine how Florida real estate is passed in a probate and vice versa, which is why probate in both states would be necessary; having all probate assets in a trust completely avoids probate.

CHAPTER 9

WHAT STEPS DO YOU TAKE TO HELP CLIENTS WITH SETTING UP THEIR LONG-TERM CARE PLAN?

For a snowbird who is making a long-term care plan, the important consideration is in which state they will enter a nursing home, and how they will pay for it. High-net-worth clients might pay out of pocket for nursing home care, while other clients might have long-term care insurance, but many people rely on Medicaid to pay for it, because nursing home care is very expensive. In New York and Florida, nursing home care can cost over $10,000 per month; with an average stay of well over one year, the bills add up quickly, and the assets can dissipate quickly. The unfortunate reality is that without proper long term care planning, the assets that you have worked your entire life to accumulate will go to pay for your care, rather than go to your heirs. Some people are okay with their assets going to pay for their care and some people are vehemently opposed to it. If you are vehemently opposed to your assets going to pay for your long term care, then long term care planning is essential to ensure you can both safeguard your assets for the next generation and qualify for Medicaid to pay for your long term care. Of course, being a snowbird can add some complexity to this.

Medicaid is a means tested program, meaning you must meet certain income and asset criteria to qualify. In order for a person to qualify Medicaid to pay for nursing home care, an individual must impoverish themselves to a certain level, depending on whether they are in Florida or New York.

A full explanation of Medicaid planning could fill its own book, but a bread-and-butter aspect of Medicaid planning in New York is the transfer of ones house at least five years prior to making an application for Medicaid. The purpose of transferring the house is to remove the house from counting as the person's asset for Medicaid purposes. This helps in two ways, one the house value may otherwise disqualify the person for Medicaid and two, if the house is not your asset, then upon your passing Medicaid cannot go after it to recoup the medical expenses paid on your behalf. The reason the transfer needs to be made at least five years prior to a Medicaid application is that there is a "five year look back period" wherein Medicaid can impose a penalty period for transfers made within five years of your application. The simplest strategy to avoid any penalty period is to make transfers more than five years before making a Medicaid application.

In Florida on the other hand, if you are a Florida resident you may elect a homestead exemption on your primary residence. The homestead exemption would allow the house to pass to your heirs free from creditor claims, including Medicaid. However, you can only claim the homestead exemption for your primary residence. So, New York residents cannot claim the homestead exemption for their Florida homes, nor can a Florida resident claim the homestead exemption for multiple homes. For this reason it is prudent to consider creating a special type of irrevocable trust called a "Medicaid trust."

The Medicaid type trust will be irrevocable, so unlike your revocable trust, once the house is in the trust it cannot come back out to you. You retain the right to live in the house for your lifetime and your spouse can live in the house for his or her lifetime as well. Upon the second of you and your spouse to die, or upon your death if you do not have a spouse, the house would pass via the terms of the trust. The benefit to the trust is that after five years, whether you are in New York or Florida the property in the trust is no longer considered your property for purposes of qualifying for Medicaid. If you want to sell your house, the trust would sell the house and the proceeds of the sale would stay in the trust. If the house is sold, again only at your direction, the trust would contain language that directs the trustee to purchase a new house of your choosing with the trust assets. If the trust generated any income, that income would be paid to you. So, if you rent out your house for the summer, you would get the rental income. The only thing that cannot be returned to you is the trust principal. So, again, if the house is sold the sales proceeds would remain in the trust. Even if you sell the house in the trust to downsize to a less expensive house the additional money in the trust must remain in the trust.

Since Florida has a homestead exemption, a house owned by a Florida resident doesn't necessarily need to be transferred to a trust. With that said, it's a good idea for a snowbird to have both their New York and Florida residences in an irrevocable Medicaid trust so that no matter where they end up making a Medicaid application, their houses will not be included. In essence, it helps a person to artificially impoverish themselves.

How Might Changing The Domicile Impact Medicaid And Other Long-Term Care Planning From New York To Florida?

Changing your domicile is not going to have much of an effect on a long-term care plan, because both New York and Florida are pretty liberal in terms of people moving to one or the other state and qualifying for Medicaid. It's not much of a question of becoming a New York resident or becoming a Florida resident so much as it is a question of having done the proper planning for a New York application or Florida application to be successful and safe guard your assets.

What Should Be Considered When It Comes To Long-Term Care Planning?

When doing long-term care planning, the most important factor is putting the house(s) into an irrevocable Medicaid trust. Once the five-year lookback period has passed in New York, the house(s) would not be included in the Medicaid application as an asset. In New York, a certain portion of the equity in the house(s) will be considered an exempt asset, but the problem is that upon the individual's passing, the state becomes a creditor that can put a claim against the estate, and potentially put a lien against the house as an asset to recover any expenses they paid on the deceased's behalf; all of this can be avoided by putting the house(s) in a trust.

Moving a house into a trust doesn't really affect the day-to-day life of the owner of the house, because they will still get the property tax exemption (Homestead exemption or STAR discount), and will still be able to do almost anything they want with the house, such as renovate it or ask the trustee to sell it. The only drawback is that if the house is sold, the individual would not be able to get the proceeds, since the trustee can only distribute the trust income, not the trust principal. Again, this means that if the individual were to rent their house, they would be able to get the income from the renters, but if they were to sell their house, they would not get the proceeds from the sale. This brings me to a very important point, which is that if someone puts their house in a Medicaid trust, they should not be relying upon the equity in that house to fund their retirement. This is because if the house is sold, the proceeds of the sale of the house will have to remain in the trust.

There isn't necessarily a minimum or maximum age for considering Medicaid planning, but there is certainly an age range during which it makes the most sense, which is when a person is more than five years away from having to go into a nursing home. This means that if a person feels like they may need to enter a nursing home within a couple of years and they have not done any Medicaid planning, then they have probably waited too long. On the other hand, if a person doesn't think they will need to enter a nursing home for another 30 years and they have already done Medicaid planning, then they probably did it too early. Prior to doing Medicaid planning, a person should be settled financially and able to move their house(s) into a trust while still being able to fund their retirement.

CHAPTER 10

THREE TIER ESTATE PLANNING FOR SNOWBIRDS SUMMARY

As I stated earlier, I consider snowbird estate planning to be in three tiers.

The first tier affects every snowbird, whether you rent or own your home, whether you live in a mobile home while in Florida or a house with ocean views, whether you spend two months or ten months in Florida, and that is having the basic estate planning documents for New York and Florida. Every snowbird should have a: 1. Last Will and Testament; 2. Health Care Proxy (Declaration of Health Care Surrogate); 3. Living Will (Declaration); and 4. Durable Power of Attorney. People who divide their time between New York and Florida should have versions of these documents for both states.

Unlike a Will, which you can only have one of, you can have a Health Care Proxy, a Living Will and a Durable Power of Attorney for New York and have their Florida equivalents, and both the New York documents and Florida documents would be valid and in effect. Snowbirds should keep their New York documents in New York and bring their Florida documents to Florida.

The second tier affects every snowbird who owns their home in both New York and Florida, or who owns real estate in multiple states, and that is planning to avoid probate and ancillary probate. Why do we hate probate? Because it is expensive, time consuming, and out of our control (because a judge is overseeing the probate). Is there anything worse than probate? Yes, ancillary probate. Ancillary probate occurs when a snowbird owns real estate in two states, and based on the constitutional doctrine of sovereignty between the states, one state cannot direct how real estate in another state shall pass. So, probate is necessary in all states where you own real estate. Ancillary probate can be avoided by creating a revocable trust and transferring all out of state property to that trust. Even better, transfer all probate property to the revocable trust and avoid probate entirely.

The third tier of snowbird estate planning is Domicile, or what state considers you to be a resident for tax purposes. Tier three affects snowbirds of two types, those who are higher net worth individuals that can benefit from Florida not taxing its residents income or estates, or those snowbirds who are planning on using Medicaid for their long term care.

If you decide to change your domicile to Florida for tax purposes, you should be aware that New York is very aggressive in conducting residency audits, which can be fact intensive. The best way to establish that you are domiciled in Florida is to actually move your life to Florida, i.e. spend most of your time in Florida, maintain a residence nicer or equal to your New York residence, change all licensing and registrations to Florida, move your important things to Florida, and begin maintaining your life down there and come to New York for visits, rather than the other way around. Also, you should be prepared for a residency audit by maintaining your evidence that you are domiciled in Florida and that you spend less than 183 days per year in New York.

If you are considering changing your domicile to Florida for long term care purposes the key to remember is there is a five year look back on transfers no matter where you apply for Medicaid. So, it is important to consider where you may need long term care and when and to plan well in advance.

CHAPTER 11

HOW DOES YOUR FIRM STAY ON TOP OF CHANGING LAWS IN BOTH STATES?

I'm an active member of the New York State Bar Association and the Florida Bar Association, and I stay on top of all estate tax and estate planning issues. I frequently write articles for my firm's blog, and for my own website on estate planning at snowbirdestateplanning.com. Many of the articles on that website address the latest changes in New York and Florida related to snowbird estate planning.

Can Any Estate Planning Attorney Help Set Up Our Estate Planning Documents For Both New York And Florida?

It is extremely beneficial to hire an attorney who is well-versed in the differences between Florida and New York law as they relate to estate planning for snowbirds. This is an ever-changing field of law, so it is best to have an attorney who is admitted to practice and can represent their clients in both states.

A lot of parents say to their kids, "Call my estate planning attorney if anything ever happens to me, because they have all my documents and will be able to help you." The problem is that if the parent passes away in Florida, for instance, a New York estate planning attorney will only be able to help if they are also admitted in Florida. That is not going to help one's heirs; what will help is having an attorney who is admitted to practice in both New York and Florida, so that the attorney can represent them regardless of where they need to do a probate or administer the trust.

In addition, a New York and Florida attorney will be aware of the latest changes in both New York and Florida law. An attorney who can only practice in New York might unknowingly give their snowbird client a health care proxy form that is outdated. In fact, the power of attorney form in Florida was changed in 2017, and I often encounter people who have previously worked with attorneys that instructed them to use that outdated form. Snowbirds need an attorney who understands the differences between New York and Florida law, and can guide them accordingly.

What Is It That Truly Sets You And Your Firm Apart When It Comes To Multi-State Estate Planning And Long-Term Planning Needs?

I am admitted to practice in both New York and Florida, so I can represent clients in both states. I have an LLM in taxation from NYU, which is an advanced degree that helps me do advanced estate tax planning for high-net-worth individuals. There are 10 estate planning attorneys at my firm, each of which focus on a particular sub-topic within estate planning, which means for the client, we really can be a "one-stop-shop," for lack of a better term. We have attorneys who just do long-term care planning day in and day out, and we have attorneys who just do estate administration day in and day out.

When clients hire our firm, they aren't going to get a jack-of-all trades attorney; they're going to have access to multiple attorneys who focus on specific areas within estate planning law. We are also a full-service firm, so if a client has a business issue, tax issue, real estate transaction, immigration issue, matrimonial issue, or employment law issue, just to name a few, we can offer attorneys who specialize in each, and those attorneys are highly experienced in what they do.

APPENDIX

Durable Powers of Attorney

New York Durable Power of Attorney form

POWER OF ATTORNEY
NEW YORK STATUTORY SHORT FORM

(a) CAUTION TO THE PRINCIPAL: *Your Power of Attorney is an important document. As the "principal," you give the person whom you choose (your "agent") authority to spend your money and sell or dispose of your property during your lifetime without telling you. You do not lose your authority to act even though you have given your agent similar authority.*

When your agent exercises this authority, he or she must act according to any instructions you have provided or, where there are no specific instructions, in your best interest. "Important Information for the Agent" at the end of this document describes your agent's responsibilities.

Your agent can act on your behalf only after signing the Power of Attorney before a notary public.

You can request information from your agent at any time. If you are revoking a prior Power of Attorney, you should provide written notice of the revocation to your prior agent(s) and to any third parties who may have acted upon it, including the financial institutions where your accounts are located.

You can revoke or terminate your Power of Attorney at any time for any reason as long as you are of sound mind. If you are no longer of sound mind, a court can remove an agent for acting improperly.

Your agent cannot make health care decisions for you. You may execute a "Health Care Proxy" to do this.

The law governing Powers of Attorney is contained in the New York General Obligations Law, Article 5, Title 15. This law is available at a law library, or online through the New York State Senate or Assembly websites, www.nysenate.gov or www.nyassembly.gov.

If there is anything about this document that you do not understand, you should ask a lawyer of your own choosing to explain it to you.

(b) DESIGNATION OF AGENT(S):

I, **[PRINCIPAL]**, residing at [ADDRESSP], hereby appoint:

[AGENT1], residing at [ADDRESSA1], as my agent(s).

If you designate more than one agent above and you do not initial the statement below, they must act together.

(   ) My agents may act SEPARATELY.

(c) DESIGNATION OF SUCCESSOR AGENT(S): (OPTIONAL)
If any agent designated above is unable or unwilling to serve, I appoint as my successor agent(s):

[AGENT2], residing at [ADDRESSA2] and **[AGENT3],** residing at [ADDRESSA3].

If you do not initial the statement below, successor agents designated above must act together.

(   ) My successor agents may act SEPARATELY.

Page 1 of 9 Pages

You may provide for specific succession rules in this section. Insert specific succession provisions here:

(d) This POWER OF ATTORNEY shall not be affected by my subsequent incapacity unless I have stated otherwise below, under "Modifications".

(e) This POWER OF ATTORNEY DOES NOT REVOKE any Powers of Attorney previously executed by me unless I have stated otherwise below, under "Modifications."

(f) GRANT OF AUTHORITY:

To grant your agent some or all of the authority below, either

(1) Initial the bracket at each authority you grant, or

(2) Write or type the letters for each authority you grant on the blank line at (P), and initial the bracket at (P). If you initial (P), you do not need to initial the other lines.

I grant authority to my agent(s) with respect to the following subjects as defined in sections 5-1502A through 5-1502N of the New York General Obligations Law:

( ) (A) real estate transactions;

( ) (B) chattel and goods transactions;

( ) (C) bond, share, and commodity transactions;

( ) (D) banking transactions;

( ) (E) business operating transactions;

( ) (F) insurance transactions;

( ) (G) estate transactions;

( ) (H) claims and litigation;

( ) (I) personal and family maintenance: If you grant your agent this authority, it will allow the agent to make gifts that you customarily have made to individuals, including the agent, and charitable organizations. The total amount of all such gifts in any one calendar year cannot exceed five thousand dollars;

( ) (J) benefits from governmental programs or civil or military service;

( ) (K) financial matters related to health care; records, reports, and statements;

( ) (L) retirement benefit transactions;

( ) (M) tax matters;

( ) (N) all other matters;

( ) (O) full and unqualified authority to my agent(s) to delegate any or all of the foregoing powers to any person or persons whom my agent(s) select;

( ) (P) EACH of the matters identified by the following letters (A) through and including (O).

You need not initial the other lines if you initial line (P).

(g) CERTAIN GIFT TRANSACTIONS: (OPTIONAL)

In order to authorize your agent to make gifts in excess of an annual total of $5,000 for all gifts

Page 2 of 9 Pages

described in (I) of the grant of authority section of this document (under personal and family maintenance), and/or to make changes to interest in your property, you must expressly grant that authorization in the Modifications section below. If you wish to authorize your agent to make gifts to himself or herself, you must expressly grant such authorization in the Modifications section below. Granting such authority to your agent gives your agent the authority to take actions which could significantly reduce your property and/or change how your property is distributed at your death. Your choice to grant such authority should be discussed with a lawyer.

( ) I grant my agent authority to make gifts in accordance with the terms and conditions of the Modifications that supplement this Statutory Power of Attorney.

(h) MODIFICATIONS: (OPTIONAL)

In this section, you may make additional provisions, including, but not limited to, language to limit or supplement authority granted to your agent, language to grant your agent the specific authority to make gifts to himself of herself, and /or language to grant your agent the specific authority to make other gift transactions and/or changes to interests in your property. Your agent is entitled to be reimbursed from your assets for reasonable expenses incurred on your behalf. In this section, you may make additional provisions if you ALSO wish your agent(s) to be compensated from your assets for services rendered on your behalf, and you may define "reasonable compensation."

STANDARD MODIFICATIONS

( ) (A) enter any safe deposit box or other place of safekeeping standing in the name of the principal alone or jointly with another and to remove the contents of the principal and make additions, substitutions or replacements of the contents of the principal;

( ) (B) prepare, execute and file income, gift and other tax returns required by the laws of the United States or of any state or subdivision thereof, to confer with revenue agents, execute and file refund claims, collect any tax refunds, execute agreements extending the statute of limitations, represent the principal or obtain representation for the principal before the Tax Court of the United States or any other court in connection with all income, gift or other tax matters; sign federal Form 2848 and any similar state form as may be necessary and permissible by the taxing authority;

( ) (C) represent the principal in all matters before the Social Security Administration, any state Medicaid agency, or any other governmental agency in charge of benefits and entitlement programs, including, but not limited to, the power to make an application for benefits, and appeal the denial, reduction or discontinuation of benefits;

( ) (D) represent the principal in all matters before any governmental agency, board or tribunal on the federal, state or local level;

( ) (E) exercise all statutory elections against the estate or property of any person from which such right is derived;

( ) (F) exercise my rights over and/or make decisions pertaining to my retirement plans, including individual retirement accounts, rollovers and voluntary contributions; to apply for and receive benefits thereunder; to designate or alter designated beneficiaries of ERISA and/or all other retirement plans;

( ) (G) exercise all rights which the principal may have in any life, health and long-term care insurance policy, including, but not limited to, the power to collect proceeds from, the right to borrow against, surrender, or assign said policy, to designate or change the designated beneficiary thereof, to exercise any options under said policy, and to transfer ownership thereof;

( ) (H) create, amend, revoke or terminate any inter vivos trusts, whether revocable or irrevocable, on behalf of the principal; to fund such trusts on behalf of the principal or to make transfers and additions to any trusts already in existence, in a manner consistent with my estate plan;

( ) (I) exercise any limited/special power of appointment held by the principal;

( ) (J) lend or borrow on such terms and with such security as my agent may decide in his sole discretion and to execute all notes, mortgages and other instruments relating to such;

( ) (K) to change or maintain my abode, domicile or residency for any and all purposes, including placement in an assisted living facility or skilled nursing facility, should that be necessary, and to take any and all actions to effectuate the foregoing, including but not limited to, executing a Declaration of Intent to Return Home;

( ) (L) serve as the guardian of my person and property, to serve without bond, in the event that I shall be declared unable to manage my affairs pursuant to Article 81 of the Mental Hygiene Law of the State of New York or any statute corresponding thereto;

( ) (M) enter into buy/sell agreements, personal services contracts or any other contract or arrangement on my behalf with any person including my agent;

( ) (N) retain, discharge, and pay for the services of attorneys, accountants, financial planners, geriatric care managers, social workers and other health care professionals;

( ) (O) This power of attorney revokes all powers of attorney I have previously executed;

( ) (P) If any provision herein is deemed invalid, such provision shall not affect the validity of other provisions herein;

( ) (Q) Shall have the same powers and rights that the principal possesses over all the principal's "digital assets", as hereinafter defined, including, but not limited to: (i) the power to access, use, take control of, transfer and dispose of the principal's "digital devices" as hereinafter defined for the purpose of accessing, using, modifying, deleting, controlling, transferring, disposing, or otherwise dealing with the principal's digital assets, and (ii) the power to access, use, modify, delete, control, transfer, dispose, and otherwise deal with the principal's digital assets. Digital assets shall include, but not be limited to, all files stored on any digital devices, email accounts, digital storage accounts, digital music accounts, digital documents, digital audio accounts, digital photograph accounts, digital video accounts, software licenses, social media accounts, file sharing accounts, domain registrations and domain name system (DNS) service accounts, web hosting accounts, tax preparation service accounts, financial management accounts, online store accounts, affiliate program accounts, other online accounts and similar digital items which currently exist or may exist as technology develops or such comparable items as technology develops. For all purposes, digital devices shall include, but not be limited to desktops, laptops, tablets, peripherals, storage devices, backup systems, mobile telephones, smartphones, and other similar digital device which currently exists or may exist as technology develops or such comparable items as technology develops.

( ) (R) each of the above matters identified by the letters: (A) through and including (Q).

ADDITIONAL MODIFICATIONS

My agent(s) or successor agent(s) shall have the authority over each matter below where I have placed my initials.

( ) (A) make gifts of any amount, in cash or in kind, on my behalf to any person or persons, in a manner consistent with my estate plan;

( ) (B) make gifts to any charitable organization customarily made by the principal;

( ) (C) I grant authority to my agent to make gifts to my spouse, children and more remote descendants, and parents, which the agent reasonably deems to be in my best interest unlimited in amount;

( ) (D) disclaim in whole or in part, any interest or power passing to the principal by will or by intestate succession or by any other means;

( ) (E) open, modify, withdraw from, deposit to or terminate a deposit account in the name of the principal and other joint tenants;

( ) (F) open, modify, withdraw from, deposit to or terminate any other joint account in the name of the principal and other joint tenants;

( ) (G) open, modify, withdraw from, deposit to or terminate a bank account in trust form as described in Section 7-5.1 of the Estates, Powers and Trusts Law, and designate or change the beneficiary or beneficiaries of such account;

( ) (H) open, modify, withdraw from, deposit to or terminate a transfer on death account as described in Part Four of Article Thirteen of the Estates, Powers and Trusts Law, and designate and/or change the beneficiary or beneficiaries of such account;

( ) (I) exercise all rights which the principal may have in any annuity contract, including but not limited to changing the beneficiary or beneficiaries of any annuity contract for the benefit of the principal and/or assign or transfer ownership of said annuity contract;

( ) (J) procure new, different or additional contracts of insurance on the life of the principal or annuity contracts for the benefit of the principal and designate the beneficiary or beneficiaries of any such contract;

( ) (K) open, modify, terminate or transfer a custodial account or tuition savings account or prepaid tuition plan as defined under Section 529 of the Internal Revenue Code, including the right to name successor custodian(s) or owner thereto;

( ) (L) create, change or terminate other property interests or rights of survivorship, and designate or change the beneficiary or beneficiaries therein;

( ) (M) to prepare, execute, consent to on behalf of the principal, and file any return, report, declaration or other document required by the laws of the United States, or by any state or political subdivision thereof, or by any foreign country or political subdivision thereof, which the agent deems to be desirable or necessary with respect to any gift made under the authority of this section;

( ) (N) to execute, acknowledge, seal and deliver any deed, assignment, agreement, trust agreement, authorization, check or other instrument which the agent deems useful for the accomplishment of any of the purposes enumerated in this section;

( ) (O) to prosecute, defend, submit to alternative dispute resolution, settle and propose or accept a compromise with respect to any claim existing in favor of or against the principal based on or involving any gift transaction or to intervene in any related action or proceeding;

( ) (P) in general, and in addition to but not in contravention of all the specific acts listed in this section, to do any other act or acts which the agent deems desirable or necessary to complete any such gift on behalf of the principal;

( ) (Q) A gift or other transfer of property may be made outright, by exercise or release of a presently exercisable general or special power of appointment held by the principal, to a trust established or created for such individual, to a Uniform Transfers to Minors Act account for such individual (regardless of who is the custodian), or to a tuition savings account or prepaid tuition plan as defined under Section 529 of the Internal Revenue Code for the benefit of such individual (without regard to who is the account owner or responsible individual for such account);

( ) (R) In making gifts of my property, my "best interest" shall include gifts which would be likely to cause a reduction in estate tax due or which would carry out a plan for the protection of my assets against the costs of nursing home care in the foreseeable future;

( ) (S) I grant specific authority for the following agent(s) to make the following gifts to himself or herself: **[AGENT1]** and **[AGENT2]**. Gifts to the agents under this provision include all the powers, methods and manners as provided for gifting above.

( ) (T) I grant the authority to my agent(s) or successor agent(s) to make gifts or transfers pursuant to my instructions or as my agent reasonably deems to be in my best interest for each of the matters identified by the letter (A) through and including (S) above.

COMPENSATION MODIFICATION

(   ) The agent(s) shall be compensated for services in handling my financial affairs at the same rate as that of an executor or administrator of an estate and may pay said compensation from the funds in his/her hands following the close of each calendar year or more frequently. The commission shall be calculated upon the amount of money received by him/her as income and upon income paid out, whether such income is derived from the corpus of the estate or from any other source, and also a commission for receiving and paying out corpus of the estate paid out during the period. The commissions on income and principal shall commence each year at the initial bracket. If agent is an attorney and performs any legal services for me, agent shall be entitled to reasonable attorney's fees apart from and in addition to the compensation provided for herein.

(i) DESIGNATION OF MONITOR(S): (OPTIONAL)

If you wish to appoint monitor(s), initial and fill in the section below:

(   ) I wish to designate ___________________, whose address(es) is (are) ______________________, as monitor(s). Upon the request of the monitor(s), my agent(s) must provide the monitor(s) with a copy of the power of attorney and a record of all transactions done or made on my behalf. Third parties holding records of such transactions shall provide the records to the monitor(s) upon request.

(j) COMPENSATION OF AGENT(S):

Your agent is entitled to be reimbursed from your assets for reasonable expenses incurred on your behalf. If you ALSO wish your agent(s) to be compensated from your assets for services rendered on your behalf, and/or you wish to define "reasonable compensation", you may do so above, under "Modifications".

(k) ACCEPTANCE BY THIRD PARTIES:

I agree to indemnify the third party for any claims that may arise against the third party because of reliance on this Power of Attorney. I understand that any termination of this Power of Attorney, whether the result of my revocation of the Power of Attorney or otherwise, is not effective as to a third party until the third party has actual notice or knowledge of the termination.

(l) TERMINATION:

This Power of Attorney continues until I revoke it or it is terminated by my death or other event described in section 5-1511 of the General Obligations Law.

Section 5-1511 of the General Obligations Law describes the manner in which you may revoke your Power of Attorney, and the events which terminate the Power of Attorney.

(m) SIGNATURE AND ACKNOWLEDGMENT:

In Witness Whereof I have hereunto signed my name on _____________, 20__

PRINCIPAL signs here: ====> ________________________________

[PRINCIPAL]

STATE OF NEW YORK)ss:
COUNTY OF ____________)

On the ____ day of _________, 20__, before me, the undersigned, personally appeared **[PRINCIPAL]**, personally known to me or proved to me on the basis of satisfactory evidence to be the individual whose name is subscribed to the within instrument and acknowledged to me that he/she executed the same in his/her capacity, and that by his/her signature on the instrument, the individual, or the person upon behalf of which the individual acted, executed the instrument.

____
Notary Public

(n) SIGNATURE OF WITNESSES:

By signing as a witness, I acknowledge that the principal signed the Power of Attorney in my presence and in the presence of the other witness, or that the principal acknowledged to me that the principal's signature was affixed by him or her or at his or her direction. I also acknowledge that the principal has stated that this Power of Attorney reflects his or her wishes and that he or she has signed it voluntarily. I am not named herein as an agent or as a permissible recipient of gifts.

_______________________	_______________________
Signature of Witness 1	*Signature of Witness 2*
_______________________	_______________________
Date	*Date*
_______________________	_______________________
Print Name	*Print Name*
_______________________	_______________________
Address	*Address*
_______________________	_______________________
City, State, Zip Code	*City, State, Zip Code*

(o) IMPORTANT INFORMATION FOR THE AGENT:

When you accept the authority granted under this Power of Attorney, a special legal relationship is created between you and the principal. This relationship imposes on you legal responsibilities that continue until you resign or the Power of Attorney is terminated or revoked. You must:

(1) act according to any instructions from the principal, or, where there are no instructions, in the principal's best interest;

(2) avoid conflicts that would impair your ability to act in the principal's best interest;

Page 7 of 9 Pages

(3) keep the principal's property separate and distinct from any assets you own or control, unless otherwise permitted by law;

(4) keep a record of all transactions conducted for the principal or keep all receipts of payments and transactions conducted for the principal; and

(5) disclose your identity as an agent whenever you act for the principal by writing or printing the principal's name and signing your own name as "agent" in either of the following manners: (Principal's Name) by (Your Signature) as Agent, or (your signature) as Agent for (Principal's Name).

You may not use the principal's assets to benefit yourself or anyone else or make gifts to yourself or anyone else unless the principal has specifically granted you that authority in the modifications section of this document or a Non-Statutory Power of Attorney. If you have that authority, you must act according to any instructions of the principal or, where there are no such instructions, in the principal's best interest.

You may resign by giving written notice to the principal and to any co-agent, successor agent, monitor if one has been named in this document, or the principal's guardian if one has been appointed. If there is anything about this document or your responsibilities that you do not understand, you should seek legal advice.

Liability of agent: The meaning of the authority given to you is defined in New York's General Obligations Law, Article 5, Title 15. If it is found that you have violated the law or acted outside the authority granted to you in the Power of Attorney, you may be liable under the law for your violation.

(p) AGENT'S SIGNATURE AND ACKNOWLEDGMENT OF APPOINTMENT:

It is not required that the principal and the agent(s) sign at the same time, nor that multiple agents sign at the same time.

I/we, **[AGENT1]**, have read the foregoing Power of Attorney. I am/we are the person(s) identified therein as agent(s) for the principal named therein.

I/we acknowledge my/our legal responsibilities.

In Witness Whereof I have hereunto signed my name on ______________________ 20__

Agent(s) sign(s) here: ==> ____
[AGENT1]

==> ____

STATE OF NEW YORK)ss:
COUNTY OF ____________)

On the _____ day of ___________, 20__, before me, the undersigned, personally appeared **[AGENT1]**, personally known to me or proved to me on the basis of satisfactory evidence to be the individual whose name is subscribed to the within instrument and acknowledged to me that he/she executed the same in his/her capacity, and that by his/her signature on the instrument, the individual, or the person upon behalf of which the individual acted, executed the instrument.

____
Notary Public

STATE OF NEW YORK)ss:
COUNTY OF ____________)

On the _____ day of ___________, 20__, before me, the undersigned, personally appeared ___________________, personally known to me or proved to me on the basis of satisfactory evidence to be the individual whose name is subscribed to the within instrument and acknowledged to me that he/she executed the same in his/her capacity, and that by his/her signature on the instrument, the individual, or the person upon behalf of which the individual acted, executed the instrument.

____
Notary Public

(q) SUCCESSOR AGENT'S SIGNATURE AND ACKNOWLEDGMENT OF APPOINTMENT:

It is not required that the principal and the SUCCESSOR agent(s), if any, sign at the same time, nor that multiple SUCCESSOR agents sign at the same time. Furthermore, successor agents can not use this power of attorney unless the agent(s) designated above is/are unable or unwilling to serve.

I/we, **[AGENT2]**, have read the foregoing Power of Attorney. I am/we are the person(s) identified therein as SUCCESSOR agent(s) for the principal named therein.

In Witness Whereof I have hereunto signed my name on _______________________ 20__

Successor Agent(s) sign(s) here: ==> _____________________________________
[AGENT2]

==> _____________________________________

STATE OF NEW YORK)ss:
COUNTY OF ____________)

On the _____ day of __________, 20___, before me, the undersigned, personally appeared **[AGENT2]**, personally known to me or proved to me on the basis of satisfactory evidence to be the individual whose name is subscribed to the within instrument and acknowledged to me that he/she executed the same in his/her capacity, and that by his/her signature on the instrument, the individual, or the person upon behalf of which the individual acted, executed the instrument.

____
Notary Public

Florida Durable Power of Attorney form

DURABLE POWER OF ATTORNEY

I, **[PRINCIPAL]**, as of this ___ day of _______, 20__, hereby appoint and empower **[AGENT1]** as my true and lawful attorney-in-fact ("my Agent"), to act for me and in my name and on my behalf to exercise the powers listed in this instrument. Except as otherwise provided in the Florida Power of Attorney Act (Fla. Stat. Ch. 709), my Agent may exercise these powers independently and without the approval of any court. My Agent, however, shall exercise all powers in a fiduciary capacity in good faith, as a prudent person would, using reasonable care, skill, and caution. In the event **[AGENT1]** fails or ceases to act as my attorney-in-fact for any reason, I appoint **[AGENT2]** as my Agent. I hereby revoke all prior powers of attorney previously executed by me.

Third Parties. Any third party to whom this power of attorney is presented may rely upon an affidavit by my Agent stating, to the best of my Agent's knowledge and belief, that this power has not been revoked, that I am then living, and that no proceedings have been initiated to determine my incapacity. No third party relying on this power and that affidavit will be liable for any losses, damages, or claims caused by compliance with the action requested by my Agent, unless that third party has actual knowledge of my death or the revocation of this power.

A THIRD PARTY WHO IMPROPERLY REFUSES TO ACCEPT THIS POWER OF ATTORNEY WILL BE LIABLE FOR DAMAGES, INCLUDING REASONABLE ATTORNEY'S FEES AND COSTS, INCURRED IN ANY ACTION OR PROCEEDING THAT CONFIRMS THE VALIDITY OF THIS POWER OF ATTORNEY.

Durable Power. This durable power of attorney will not be affected by my subsequent incapacity except as provided in Chapter 709 of the Florida Statutes. It is my specific intent that the power conferred on my Agent will be exercisable from the date of this instrument, notwithstanding my subsequent disability or incapacity, except as otherwise specifically provided by statute.

My Agent will have the following powers and duties:

GENERAL AUTHORITY

1. To manage all assets and properties belonging to me or in which I have any interest, and to expend whatever funds my Agent deems proper for the preservation, maintenance, or improvement of those assets or properties.

2. To exercise all powers even though my Agent may also be acting individually or on behalf of any other person or entity interested in the same matters (as more fully set forth in the Additional Provisions section).

3. To seek on my behalf the assistance of a court or other governmental agency to carry out an act authorized in this power of attorney and to enforce the exercise of these powers granted to my Agent.

4. To execute, acknowledge, seal, deliver, file, or record any instrument or communication the Agent considers desirable to accomplish a purpose of a transaction, including creating at any time a schedule listing some or all of my property and attaching it to the power of attorney;

5. To exercise any authority reasonably necessary to give effect to an express grant of specific authority in this power of attorney.

6. To the extent not limited under the law of the jurisdiction in which this power of attorney is presented, to take all other actions as may be necessary or appropriate for my personal well-being and the management of my affairs, as fully and as effectively as if made or done by me personally.

REAL PROPERTY

To manage and conserve any real property, or any interest or incidents in real property, on my behalf as stated below. Such property and incidents in property include any interest in homestead property, mineral rights, and cooperative apartments. I give my Agent the following powers:

7. To receive, buy, sell, exchange, lease, encumber, and convey such property; to impose restrictions and covenants; to grant options, releases, and easements, including for public use; to adjust boundaries; and to partition or consent to partitioning, subdivide, apply for zoning or other governmental permits, plat or consent to platting, and engage in development activities for such property.

8. To pay or contest any taxes due on such property, and to receive refunds.

9. To engage in any form of litigation regarding the possession, ownership or liability involving such property, including foreclosure on a mortgage, or enforcement of a contract for sale (including specific performance).

10. To create or receive a security interest in such property, and to satisfy a mortgage.

11. To lease or sublease such property; any such lease will be valid and binding for its full term even if it extends beyond the duration of this power of attorney.

12. To insure the property against liability or casualty or other loss, and to maintain, repair or alter such property, including removing or erecting structures on the property.

13. If not prohibited in this instrument, to change the form of title of such property, including contribution into a business entity in exchange for an interest in that entity.

14. To join with other persons with whom I own property as joint tenants with right of survivorship or as tenants by the entireties in any transaction regarding that property.

15. With respect to income-producing real property, my Agent will have the powers:

    a. To retain and operate the property for as long as advisable;

    b. To control, direct, and manage the property, determining the manner and extent of my Agent's active participation in these operations, and to hire one or more supervisors for the property;

    c. To hire and discharge employees, fix their compensation, and define their duties;

    d. To invest funds in other land holdings and to use those funds for all improvements, operations, or similar purposes;

    e. To retain any of the net earnings for working capital and other purposes as advisable in conformity with sound and efficient management; and

    f. To purchase and sell machinery, equipment, and supplies of all kinds as needed for the operation and maintenance of the property.

TANGIBLE PERSONAL PROPERTY

To manage and conserve any tangible personal property, or any interest in tangible personal property, including exempt property, on my behalf, as follows:

16. To receive, buy, sell, exchange, or otherwise dispose of such property, even if without consideration.

17. To pay or contest any taxes due on such property, and to receive refunds.

18. To engage in any form of litigation regarding the possession, ownership or liability involving such property.

19. To create or receive a security interest in or grant options regarding such property.

20. To lease or sublease such property; any such lease will be valid and binding for its full term even if it extends beyond the duration of this power of attorney.

21. To insure, store, move, maintain, repair or alter such property.

22. If not prohibited in this instrument, to change the form of title of such property, including contribution into a business entity in exchange for an interest in that entity.

23. To surrender possession of such property to me or to members of my family without liability for wear, tear, and obsolescence of the property.

INVESTMENTS

24. To invest in assets, securities, or interests in securities of any nature, whether domestic or foreign markets, including (without limit) stocks, bonds, mutual funds, index funds, or investment funds, including common trust funds, provided such securities are traded on a regulated exchange.

25. To establish or maintain and to trade in credit or margin accounts (whether secured or unsecured), and to pledge assets for that purpose.

26. To hold funds uninvested for such periods as the Agent deems prudent, and to invest in any assets the Agent deems advisable even though they are not technically recognized or specifically listed in so-called "legal lists," without responsibility for depreciation or loss on account of those investments, or because those investments are non-productive, as long as the Agent acts in good faith.

27. To trade in commodities, options, futures, precious metals, and currencies, provided such items are traded on a regulated exchange.

28. To employ a custodian or agent ("the Custodian") located anywhere within the United States, at my expense, whether or not such Custodian is an affiliate of an Agent; to register securities in the name of the Custodian or a nominee thereof without designation of fiduciary capacity; and to appoint the Custodian to perform such other ministerial functions as the Agent may direct, all as permitted in Fla. Stat. Chapter 709. While such securities are in the custody of the Custodian, the Agent will be under no obligation to inspect or verify such securities, nor will the Agent be responsible for any loss by the Custodian.

29. To employ any investment management service, financial institution, or similar organization to advise the Agent; to handle investment of my assets; and to render all accountings of funds held on my behalf under custodial, agency, or other agreements. If the Agent is an individual, these costs may be paid from my assets in addition to compensation payable to the Agent.

30. To receive and hold certificates and other evidences of ownership with respect to stocks and bonds, or to hold such securities in street certificates or in a book entry system.

31. To exercise voting rights with respect to stocks and bonds in person or by proxy, enter into voting trusts, and consent to limitations on the right to vote.

32. To the extent not limited in the Special Transactions section, to apply for, fund, modify, withdraw from, or terminate a qualified tuition plan authorized under 26

USC §529, or its successor provisions, for any qualified person, including the right to combine accounts, to transfer an account from one state to another, to redirect the investment of the account (to the extent permitted by law), or to change the designated beneficiary of the plan.

33. To conduct investment transactions as provided in Fla. Stat. §709.2208(2).

34. The powers to access, take control of, handle, conduct, continue, distribute, dispose of, or terminate my digital assets and digital accounts. The term "digital assets" means, but is not limited to, files, including but not limited to, emails, documents, images, audio, video, and similar digital files which currently exist or may exist as technology develops or such comparable items as technology develops, stored on digital devices, including, but not limited to, desktops, laptops, tablets, peripherals, storage devices, mobile telephones, smartphones, and any similar digital device which currently exists or may exist as technology develops or such comparable items as technology develops, regardless of the ownership of the physical device upon which the digital asset is stored. The term "digital accounts" means, but is not limited to, email accounts, software licenses, social network accounts, social media accounts, file sharing accounts, financial management accounts, domain registration accounts, domain name service accounts, web hosting accounts, tax preparation service accounts, online stores, affiliate programs, other online accounts which currently exist or may exist as technology develops or such comparable items as technology develops.

FINANCIAL MATTERS

35. To collect, receive, and receipt for any and all sums of money or payments due or to become due to me.

36. To continue, establish, modify, or terminate an account, credit or debit card, electronic transfer authorization, or other banking arrangement with a bank, trust company, savings and loan association, credit union, thrift company, brokerage firm, insurance company, or other financial institution selected by the Agent.

37. To make, assign, draw, endorse, discount, guarantee, and negotiate promissory notes, checks, drafts, and other negotiable or nonnegotiable paper.

38. To deposit to or withdraw from, by check, order, electronic funds transfer, wire transfer, or otherwise, money or property of mine held by a financial institution.

39. To receive statements of account, notices, and similar documents from a financial institution and act with respect to them; to contract with a financial institution for services, including renting a safe deposit box or space in a vault.

40. To enter any safe deposit box or vault on which I am a signer and withdraw or add to the contents.

41. To adjust, renew or extend the time of payment of commercial paper, a debt owed to me, a debt I owe, or a debt guaranteed by me, or any other financial transaction.

42. To borrow money on my behalf and pledge as security my personal property; to apply for, receive, and use letters of credit from a financial institution, and givc an indemnity or other agreement in connection with them.

43. To conduct banking transactions as provided in Fla. Stat. §709.2208(1).

BUSINESSES AND CONTRACTS

44. To act for me in any business or enterprise, including sole proprietorships, general or limited partnerships, joint ventures, business trusts, land trusts, limited liability companies, and other domestic and foreign forms of organizations (each referred to as an "Entity"), in which I am now or have been engaged or interested.

45. To change the form of organization or governing jurisdiction under which an Entity is operated, or its name, or any of the above, and to continue any unincorporated business that the Agent determines is not advisable to incorporate.

46. To buy, sell, enlarge or reduce my ownership interest in any Entity, and to contribute additional capital into an Entity in which I have an interest.

47. To enter into an ownership agreement with other persons to take over all or part of the operation of an Entity.

48. To establish the value of an Entity under a buy-sell agreement to which I am a party, and to enforce the terms of any agreement relating to ownership (or sale) of an interest in an Entity.

49. To participate in any type of liquidation or reorganization of any enterprise.

50. To vote and exercise all rights and options, or empower another to vote and exercise those rights and options as permitted by law, concerning any interests in an Entity, in securities, or in other assets; to enter into or approve agreements for merger, reorganization, conversion, domestication or equivalent transactions with respect to any Entity; and to enter into voting trusts and other agreements or subscriptions.

51. To exercise in person or by proxy, or enforce by litigation or otherwise, a right, power, privilege, or option I have as the holder of stocks and bonds;

52. To compromise or otherwise adjust claims in favor of or against any Entity in which I have an interest.

53. Except as otherwise provided under Fla. Stat. Chapter 709 relating to contracts for personal services, to contract with any person or Entity for any purpose, including

my attorney-in-fact in connection with a Personal Services Contract, and to perform such contract; to agree to any termination, release, rescission or modification of any contract or agreement.

54. Notwithstanding anything in this Durable Power of Attorney to the contrary, my Agent cannot bind me to any arbitration agreement with a medical, residential or health care provider.

INSURANCE, ANNUITIES, AND RETIREMENT FUNDS

For purposes of this section, a "Contract" means a contract of insurance on my life, a contract of insurance regarding my disability or long term care, or an annuity (however denominated). A "Plan" means a retirement plan or account created by an employer, by me, or by another person to provide retirement benefits or deferred compensation for me as a participant, beneficiary, or owner, including a plan or account under the following sections of the Internal Revenue Code (as amended from time to time): an individual retirement account under §§408, 408A, or 408(q); an annuity or mutual fund custodial account under §403(b); a pension, profit-sharing, stock bonus, or other retirement plan qualified under §401(a); a plan under §457(b), and a nonqualified deferred compensation plan under §409A. To the extent not limited in the Special Transactions section, I give my Agent the following powers:

55. To continue, pay the premium or make a contribution on, modify, exchange, rescind, release, or terminate a Contract, whether or not I am a beneficiary under the contract, and whether owned by me or obtained by my Agent;

56. To procure new Contracts for me and any member of my family;

57. To exercise the following rights for Contracts:

    a. To obtain a loan secured by a Contract or to borrow against its value;

    b. To surrender a Contract and receive its cash surrender value;

    c. To exercise any election available under that Contract;

    d. To exercise investment powers, if applicable;

    e. To change the manner of paying premiums and to select the form and timing of the payment of proceeds;

    f. To change or convert the Contract to another type;

    g. To sell, assign, or otherwise transfer the Contract.

58. To obtain property, casualty, liability or any other insurance for me and my property.

59. With respect to a Plan, I give my Agent the following powers:

a. To select the form and timing of payments and withdraw benefits from the Plan;

b. To make rollovers, including a direct trustee-to-trustee rollover, of benefits from one Plan to another;

c. To establish a Plan in my name;

d. To make contributions to a Plan;

e. To exercise investment powers, if applicable;

f. To borrow from, sell assets to, or purchase assets from a Plan.

ESTATES, TRUSTS, AND OTHER BENEFICIAL INTERESTS

To the extent not limited in the Special Transactions section, to act for me regarding any trust, probate estate, guardianship, conservatorship, escrow, custodianship or fund in which I may have a right or beneficial interest, including:

60. To make an election on my behalf for me to receive an elective share of my spouse's estate, if any, as provided by Florida law from time to time.

61. To exercise for my benefit a presently exercisable general power of appointment.

62. To transfer property to the trustee of a trust created by me or for my benefit.

63. To accept, receipt for, sell, assign, pledge, or exchange my interest; to reject or disclaim, or consent to a modification of, my interest.

64. To initiate and pursue litigation, including settlement, compromise, or alternative dispute resolution, regarding my interest, including a determination of the meaning, validity, or effect of a deed, Will, declaration of trust, or other instrument or transaction affecting my interest, or to remove, substitute, or surcharge a fiduciary.

CLAIMS AND LITIGATION

65. To sue in my name and behalf for the recovery of any and all sums of money or other things of value, payments due or to become due to me, or damages I have sustained or will sustain; to seek an attachment, garnishment, order of arrest, or other preliminary, provisional, or intermediate relief and use an available procedure to effect or satisfy a judgment, order, or decree; and to collect, hold and disburse any property received in satisfaction of judgments.

66. To initiate or participate in adjustments of claims, either by me or against me, including submission to alternative dispute resolution, and to settle or compromise such claims.

67. To participate and bind me in any litigation, including: to waive or accept service of process on my behalf; to appear for me; to agree to stipulations or admission of facts on my behalf (other than a representation as to my personal knowledge); to verify pleadings, seek appellate review, procure and give surety and indemnity bonds, authorize and pay for records and briefs; to receive, execute, and file a consent, waiver, release, confession of judgment, satisfaction of judgment, notice, agreement, or other instrument; and to make or accept a tender or offer of judgment.

68. To pay any and all bills, accounts, claims, and demands now or hereafter payable by me, including a judgment, award, order or settlement made in connection with a claim or litigation.

69. To assert and maintain before a court or administrative agency a claim for relief or cause of action, or to seek an injunction, specific performance, or other relief.

70. To act for me with respect to any bankruptcy or insolvency concerning me or some other person, or with respect to a reorganization or receivership which affects my interest in any property.

PERSONAL AND FAMILY MATTERS

71. To demand, obtain, review, and release to others medical records, documents, or communications protected by the patient-physician privilege, attorney-client privilege, or any similar privilege, including all records subject to, and protected by, the Health Insurance Portability and Accountability Act of 1996, as amended ("HIPAA"). I designate my Agent as my personal representative under HIPAA. My Agent may also enforce any or all of the privileges listed above.

72. To nominate on my behalf a person (including my Agent) or entity to be appointed by a court of appropriate jurisdiction as guardian of my person or property, or both, or as custodian for my property during the pendency of any proceedings to determine my legal capacity.

73. To receive and open my mail, change my mailing address, and otherwise represent me in any matter concerning the U.S. Postal Service.

74. To access communications intended for me, and communicate on my behalf, whether by mail, electronic transmission, telephone, or other means.

75. To access my accounts involving web-based communications, such as email, memberships in organizations or commercial enterprises, and social media, all of which require a user name and password for access, even to the extent of compelling

the provider to reset my information to data of my Agent's choosing.

76. To the extent not limited in the Special Transactions section, to continue or discontinue my membership in any club, religious institution, society, order, or other organization (whether individual or family) and to continue or discontinue payment of dues, fees, or contributions to those organizations.

77. Accept or resign on my behalf from any offices or positions which I may hold, including any fiduciary positions.

78. To hire and compensate attorneys, accountants, advisors, financial consultants, managers, agents, and assistants (including any individual or entity who provides investment advisory or management services, or who furnishes professional assistance in making investments) without liability for any act of those persons, if they are selected and retained with reasonable care. An Agent may serve in one or more of these capacities and be compensated separately for the services in each.

79. To discharge (with or without cause) any person hired by me (or on my behalf), by the Agent, or by any prior Agent, including but not limited to, the categories of persons named above, and physicians, nurses, care-givers, and domestics.

80. To make periodic payments of child support and other family maintenance required by a court or governmental agency or an agreement to which I am a party.

GOVERNMENT BENEFITS AND ACTIONS

This section deals with benefits or actions from or relating to any branch or department of the United States government, any state government, or any foreign government, whether or not recognized by the United States, including without limitation, the Social Security Administration, the Department of Veterans Affairs, the Internal Revenue Service, Medicare or Medicaid, and any government department providing payments or grants. I give my Agent the following powers:

81. To file or process claims, and receive payment for any amounts due me under Social Security, or as payments for retirement under the Civil Service Administration, the Railroad Retirement Act, any plan sponsored by a state (or a subdivision of a state) of the United States, or any branch of the military.

82. To enroll in, apply for, select, reject, change, amend, or discontinue, on my behalf, a benefit or program, and to receive and endorse for deposit in any account any payments that I receive from a governmental source.

83. To file or process claims, and receive payment for medical bills with all insurance companies through which I have coverage, including but not limited to Medicare and Medicaid, and to receive from Blue Cross/Blue Shield, Humana, United Health Care, CHAMPUS, Tricare, or any other insurer information obtained in the adjudication of

any claim in regard to services furnished to me under Title 18 of the Social Security Act.

84. To prepare, execute, and file a record, report, or other document to safeguard or promote my interest under a federal or state statute or regulation; to communicate with any representative or employee of a government or governmental subdivision, agency, or instrumentality, on my behalf.

TAXES

85. To represent me before any office of the Internal Revenue Service or any state agency, to receive confidential information regarding all tax matters (for my SSN ending in [SSN (Last 4 Digits)] _______________________) for all periods, whether before or after the execution of this instrument, and to make any tax elections on my behalf.

86. To prepare, sign and file any tax return on my behalf including income, gift, payroll, property, Federal Insurance Contributions Act, claims for refund and other tax returns or other tax-related documents, including receipts, offers, waivers, consents, and agreements.

87. To pay taxes due, collect refunds, post bonds, receive confidential information, and contest assessments, deficiencies, fines, or penalties determined by the Internal Revenue Service or any other taxing authority.

88. To execute on my behalf any power of attorney required by the Internal Revenue Service or other taxing authority.

SPECIAL TRANSACTIONS

Certain transactions under this power of attorney may profoundly affect my existing estate plan and therefore require a separate authorization for my Agent to engage in them. By initialing next to any items within the respective numbered paragraphs in this Special Transactions section, I grant my Agent the authority stated in that paragraph with respect to the item initialed. If I have not initialed an item, my Agent is not authorized to take that action.

89. <u>Gifts</u>. I authorize my Agent to make gifts of my property outright to, or for the benefit of, the persons specified below, including by the exercise of any presently exercisable general power of appointment which I hold or acquire. For these purposes, a gift "for the benefit of" a person includes a gift to a trust in which that person is a beneficiary, to a custodial account under a state version of the Uniform Transfers (or Gifts) to Minors Act, an ABLE account and to a tuition savings account or prepaid tuition plan as defined under Internal Revenue Code §529. Unless I have provided otherwise in this instrument, gifts made to different donees need not be equal in amount, character or timing. Reference to my spouse means

any person or persons whom I later marry. Gifts may be made only to:

_________ a) my spouse and my descendants

_________ b) **the following person(s)/entities:** ______________________________

____

____

The gifts to the persons I have specified above, if any, may be made in the following amounts:

_________ a) in an amount per donee not to exceed the annual dollar limits of the federal gift tax exclusion under Internal Revenue Code §2503(b) (annual exclusion)

_________ b) if my spouse agrees to consent to a split gift pursuant to Internal Revenue Code §2513, in an amount per donee not to exceed the aggregate annual gift tax exclusions for that donee for both my spouse and me

_________ c) if my spouse agrees to consent to a split gift pursuant to Internal Revenue Code §2513, in an amount per donee not to exceed the aggregate Applicable Exclusion Amounts for both my spouse and me

_________ d) **for estate planning purposes, in unlimited amounts**

_________ e) my Agent may NOT make any gifts of my property or exercise any powers of appointment I may hold. (I understand this limitation may have unintended or undesirable effects, but I choose it anyway.)

90. Trusts. I authorize my Agent to deal with trusts created by me, for me, on my behalf, or in connection with gifts from me to others as provided in the paragraph above authorizing gifts, as follows:

_________ a) To create, fund, and maintain an Income Trust pursuant to 42 USC §1396(d)(4)(B) in order to qualify me or retain my eligibility for Medicaid or any other public assistance benefits

_________ b) To create an inter vivos trust, whether revocable or irrevocable, in which I am a beneficiary

_________ c) To the extent permitted in the trust agreement, to amend, revoke, or terminate a trust of which I am a beneficiary, or transfer the assets of such a trust into another trust under which I am a beneficiary

__________ d) To create, amend, or revoke trusts for the benefit of others

__________ e) To participate in either judicial or nonjudicial modification of a trust as permitted in Fla. Stat. Chapter 736

91. Survivorship and Other Designations. My Agent may create or alter the nature of accounts in which I have an interest, as follows:

__________ a) To create or change rights of survivorship in accounts or other assets in which I have an interest

__________ b) To change a beneficiary designation for any accounts or financial instruments, including life insurance policies, annuities, or retirement accounts of any nature

__________ c) To waive my right to be a beneficiary of a joint and survivor annuity, including a survivor benefit under a retirement plan of any nature

92. Disclaimers. My Agent may disclaim interests in property on my behalf as follows:

__________ a) Disclaim any interest in property I might otherwise receive, either outright or in trust

__________ b) Disclaim any powers I have over property or as a beneficiary of any trusts (excluding any powers I possess in a fiduciary capacity)

__________ c) Disclaim any powers of appointment I have or may acquire, excluding any testamentary power of appointment that I currently exercise in my Last Will and Testament

ADDITIONAL PROVISIONS

Protection for Agent. I understand, acknowledge and anticipate that many of my Agent's actions taken pursuant to specific grants of authority in this instrument could involve him in conflicts of interest (created either by me or by my Agent), or call into question my Agent's apparent loyalty to me, or both. This might result from the totality of the circumstances facing the Agent at that time, or by virtue of the Agent's specific actions that might create the conflict of interest. I want my Agent to be free to act in my interest without concern over questionable lawsuits. Therefore, so long as my Agent acts in good faith, he will be protected as follows.

a. My Agent does not have an affirmative duty to act under this power of attorney and will not be liable for any claim or demand arising out of his good faith acts or omissions, except for actions or omissions resulting from my Agent's dishonesty, improper motive, or reckless indifference to the purposes of this power of attorney.

b. My Agent may have competing interests for himself or his affiliates, and I waive any express duty of loyalty imposed under Fla. Stat. §709.2114(2).

c. My Agent may have a conflict of interest as provided in Fla. Stat. §709.2116. Despite that section, my Agent may undertake a transaction on my behalf even if another party to that transaction is: (i) a business or trust controlled by my Agent, or of which an Agent, or any director, officer, or employee of a Corporate Agent, is also a director, officer, or employee; (ii) an affiliate or business associate of my Agent; or (iii) an Agent acting individually. This exception also extends to any relative of such a party.

d. I fully indemnify my Agent out of my assets and my estate for any actions brought against him, and damages he sustains, including attorneys' fees and costs, that have as a basis my Agent's actions or inactions resulting in both a claim for breach of fiduciary duty and actual damages to me or my estate, but this protection does not extend to actions or omissions resulting from my Agent's dishonesty, improper motive, or reckless indifference to the purposes of this power of attorney.

e. My Agent will not be liable for any actions by a predecessor agent if the Agent does not participate in or conceal the action. An Agent is not required to review the actions of a predecessor agent, absent actual knowledge by the Agent of wrongdoing.

Compensation and Expenses. My Agent will be entitled to reasonable compensation and reimbursement for all expenses reasonably incurred by him on my behalf.

Foreign Accounts. Despite any power granted to the Agent in this instrument or under law, my Agent may not exercise any power over, or transact any business with respect to, an account in a foreign country, as defined in 31 CFR 1010.350(c) and 1010.350(d), unless the Agent expressly and specifically accepts such authority in writing.

Delegation of Powers. My Agent may not delegate the powers given as my attorney-in-fact, except as follows:

a. To grant a transfer agent or similar person the authority to register securities in my name or the name of a nominee.

b. For investment management purposes as provided in Fla. Stat. §518.112.

c. To any other person, as may be permitted under the law of another jurisdiction in which this instrument is presented.

Suspension of Rights and Duties. All powers granted to an Agent will be suspended immediately if he or she becomes disabled. For these purposes, an Agent's disability is determined as follows:

a. If an Agent is determined to be incapacitated by a court having jurisdiction.

b. In the absence of a judicial determination, if the next named successor Agent reasonably believes that an Agent is suffering from any mental or physical incapacity that would affect his or her ability to manage my affairs, and if he or she obtains written confirmation of that opinion from that Agent's physician or other medical doctor, such person(s) shall give that Agent written notice to that effect. Upon delivery to the Agent of that written notice, all powers of that Agent as my attorney-in-fact will be suspended until his or her legal capacity is determined by a court, until his or her physician determines the Agent is no longer disabled, or until the persons entitled to give such written notice rescind it.

c. If an Agent fails to sign a release of relevant medical information necessary to determine his or her capacity, that Agent will be suspended for 30 days after the request for such a release is delivered to him or her by the persons described above. If the Agent consents to the release of relevant medical information, and is determined not to be disabled, he or she may elect to resume service as Agent by giving written notice to me and to the persons named above.

Use of Copies. As provided in Fla. Stat. §709.2106, a photocopy or electronic copy of this power is sufficient for its exercise.

Partial Invalidity. If any part of this power of attorney is declared invalid or unenforceable, that decision will not affect the validity of the remaining parts.

Limitation on actions of Agent. No Agent may participate in an action to the extent that a payment or distribution pursuant to that action would discharge a legal support obligation of that Agent. No Agent who is the insured of any insurance policy that I own may exercise any rights or have any incidents of ownership with respect to the policy, including the power to change the beneficiary, to surrender or cancel the policy, to assign the policy, to revoke any assignment, to pledge the policy for a loan, or to obtain from the insurer a loan against the surrender value of the policy. All such power is to be exercised solely by another Agent, if any.

In witness whereof, I have executed this durable power of attorney as of the date first written above.

Signed in the presence of:

_______________________________	_______________________________
Print Name:	**[PRINCIPAL]**

____

Print Name:

Two witnesses as to
[PRINCIPAL]

15

STATE OF FLORIDA
COUNTY OF _______

The foregoing instrument was acknowledged before me on _______ __, 20__, by **[PRINCIPAL]**

____
Notary Public--State of Florida
Print Notary Name: _______________
My Commission Number is: _______________
My Commission Expires: _______________

Personally Known _______________
Produced Identification _______________
Type of Identification _______________

16

Declarations of Domicile

Declaration of Domicile Bay County

DECLARATION OF DOMICILE

This is my Declaration of Domicile in the State of Florida that I am filing this day in accordance and in conformity with Section 222.17, Florida Statutes.

I hereby declare that I became a bona fide resident of the State of Florida on:

______________________(date of arrival)

I am, at the time of making this declaration, a bona fide resident of the State of Florida residing at:

____

(street and number) (city) (zip code)

which place of abode I recognize and intend to maintain as my permanent home, and if I maintain another place or places of abode in some other state or states, I hereby declare that my above-described residence and abode in the State of Florida constitutes my predominant and principal home, and I intend to continue it permanently as such.

I formerly resided at:

____

(street and number) (city) (county) (state)

and the place or places where I maintain another or other places of abode are as follows:

____

(street and number) (city) (county) (state)

____

(street and number) (city) (county) (state)

I understand that, as a legal resident of Florida: I am subject to intangible taxes; I must purchase Florida license plates for motor vehicles, if any, owned by me and/or my spouse; if I drive, I must have a Florida drivers license; if I vote, I must vote in the precint of my legal domicile, and that my estate will be probated in Florida courts.

______________________ (Signature)	______________________ (Signature)
Print Name______________________	Print Name______________________
ID Produced______________________	ID Produced______________________
( ) United States Citizen	( ) United States Citizen
( ) Citizen of______________________	( ) Citizen of______________________
Green Card #______________________ Date of Issuance______________________	Green Card #______________________ Date of Issuance______________________

STATE OF FLORIDA
COUNTY OF BAY
Sworn to and subscribed before me *UNDER OATH* this _______ day of ______________________, 20____.

____
Signature of Notary Public, State of Florida

To be filed with the Bay County Clerk of Circuit Court
Penalty for perjury: up to five (5) years in state prison and $5000.00 fine: Chapter 837.012, F.S.

Declaration of Domicile Brevard County

DECLARATION OF DOMICILE

TO THE CLERK OF THE COURT FOR BREVARD COUNTY, FLORIDA

This is my declaration of domicile in the State of Florida, that I am filing this day in accordance and in conformity with Section 222.17, Florida Statutes.

I hereby declare that I reside in and maintain a place of abode at:

____
(Street and Number)

____
(City) (County) (Zip Code)

Which place of abode I recognize and intend to maintain as my permanent home and, if I maintain another place or placed of abode in some other state or states, I hereby declare that my above-described residence and abode in the State of Florida constitutes my predominant and principal home, and I intend to continue it permanently as such.

I am, at the time of the making of this declaration, a bona fide resident of the State of Florida, residing at:

____
(Street and Number)

____
(City) (County) (Zip Code)

I formerly resided at:

____
(City) (County) (Zip Code)

and the place or places where I maintain another place or places of abode are as follows:

Spouse:
Children: Ages:

____
(Signature)

____
(Print or type name)

STATE OF FLORIDA
COUNTY OF BREVARD

The foregoing instrument was acknowledged before me this ______ day of _________________, A.D., 20____, by ________________________________, who is personally known to me or who has produced ________________________________ as identification and who ☐did ☐did not take an oath.

(SEAL)

____
Notary Public

____
Printed Name
My Commission Expires:

Declaration of Domicile Broward County

BROWARD COUNTY FLORIDA

DECLARATION OF DOMICILE

This is my declaration of domicile in the State of Florida that I am filing this day in accordance and in conformity with Section 222.17, Florida Statutes.

1. **I hereby declare that I am a bona fide resident of the State of Florida, and reside in and maintain a place of abode at:**

   ____

   Address City, State and Zip Code - County

   which place of abode I recognize and intend to maintain as my permanent home and, if I maintain another place or places of abode in some other state or states, I hereby declare that my above-described residence and abode in the State of Florida constitutes my predominant and principal home, and I intend to continue it permanently as such.

   I have been a bona fide resident of the State of Florida since the _____ day of ________________, _____.
   Date Month Year

2. **I formerly resided at:**

   ____

   Address City, State and Zip Code - County

3. **The place or places where I maintain another or other place or places of abode are as follows:**

   ____

   Address City, State and Zip Code - County

4. _______I intend to permanently continue and maintain domicile in the State of ____________________.

   _______I intend to be or become domiciled in the State of Florida.

   Optional: Also residing at this address:

   ____

   ____

   ____

Signature: ______________________________ Signature: ______________________________

Print Name ______________________________ Print Name ______________________________

STATE OF FLORIDA
COUNTY OF BROWARD

The foregoing instrument was acknowledged before me by means of [ ] physical presence or [ ] on-line notarization

this _____ day of ________________, _______ by____

who is [ ] personally known or [ ] has produced ______________________________ as identification.

Signature of Notarizing or Attesting Official____

(Notary Seal)

Declaration of Domicile Charlotte County

DECLARATION OF DOMICILE
(THIS IS NOT A HOMESTEAD EXEMPTION APPLICATION)
PENALTY FOR PERJURY - up to 20 years in state prison (Section 837.01, Florida Statutes)

TO THE CLERK OF COURTS
CHARLOTTE COUNTY, FLORIDA

This is my declaration of Domicile in the State of Florida that I am filing this day in accordance and in conformity with Section 222.17, Florida Statutes.

I was formerly a legal resident of ______________________________, ____________________ and I resided at
CITY STATE

____ however, I have changed my domicile
STREET AND NUMBER

and have been a bona fide resident of the State of Florida since the _______day of____________________,20____.

I now reside at ____Charlotte County,
STREET AND NUMBER CITY

Florida, and this statement is to be taken as my declaration of actual legal residence and permanent domicile in this State and County to the exclusion of all others, and I will comply with all requirements of legal residents of Florida.

I understand that as a legal resident of Florida: I am subject to intangible taxes; I must purchase Florida license plates for motor vehicles, if any, owned by me and/or my spouse; I must vote in the precinct of my legal domicile (if I vote), and that my estate will be probated in the Florida Courts.

____
PRINT NAME

____
SIGNATURE

____
PRINT NAME (SPOUSE)

____
SIGNATURE (SPOUSE)

____
MAILING ADDRESS

____

STATE OF FLORIDA

COUNTY OF CHARLOTTE

Sworn to (or affirmed) and subscribed before me by means of

__ physical presence or __ online notarization,
this__________ day of________________________, _____,

by____

____

who is personally known or who provided identification.

Type of I D____

____
Notary Signature

Sworn to and subscribed before me this____ day

of______________________________, 20_____.

CLERK OF THE CIRCURT COURT

____
Deputy Clerk Signature

Declaration of Domicile Collier County

DECLARATION OF DOMICILE

To the Clerk of the Circuit Court (County Comptroller) of Collier County, Florida.
This is my declaration of domicile in the State of Florida that I am filing this day in accordance and in conformity with Section 222.17, Florida Statutes.

FOR DOMICILIARIES OF THE STATE OF FLORIDA:

I hereby declare that I reside in and maintain a place of abode at:

____
(street and number)

______________________________, Florida
(city and county)

which place of abode I recognize and intend to maintain as my permanent home and, if I maintain another place or places of abode in some other state or states, I hereby declare that my above-described residence and abode in the State of Florida constitutes my predominant and principal home, and I intend to continue it permanently as such. I am, at the time of making this declaration, a bona fide resident of the State of Florida residing at:

____
(street and number)

______________________________, Florida
(city and county)

I formerly resided at:

____
(street and number)

____
(city, county and state)

and the place or places where I maintain another or other place or places of abode are as follows: (Here list street address, city, county, and state of any other place or places of abode.)

____
(Signature)

____
(Print Name)

Sworn to and subscribed before me this _______of _________________, ______

Crystal K. Kinzel
Clerk of the Circuit Court & Comptroller

____
(Signature of Deputy Clerk)

____
(Printed Name of Deputy Clerk)

____
(Signature of Notary Public, State of Florida)

____
(Print, type or stamp commissioned name of Notary Public)

Personally known _____ or Produced Identification _______
(Check One)
Type of identification produced ______________________
by means of __ physical presence or __ online notarization

(See reverse side for Domiciliaries of States Other than the State of Florida)

FOR DOMICILIARIES OF STATES OTHER THAN THE STATE OF FLORIDA:

I hereby declare that my domicile is in the State of ____________________ and that I intend to permanently continue and maintain my domicile in such state. At the time of making this declaration I am a bona fide resident of the State of ____________. My place of abode within the State of Florida, if any, is as follows: (Here list street address, city, and county of place of abode in Florida.)

(Person making declaration may also include such other and further facts with reference to any acts done or performed by such person which such person desires or intends not to be construed as evidencing any intention to establish his/her domicile within the State of Florida.)

____
(Signature)

____
(Print)

Sworn to and subscribed before me this ______of _________________, ______

Crystal K. Kinzel
Clerk of the Circuit Court & Comptroller

____
(Signature of Deputy Clerk)

____
(Printed Name of Deputy Clerk)

____
(Signature of Notary Public, State of Florida)

____
(Print, type or stamp commissioned name of Notary Public)

Personally Known _____ or Produced Identification _______by means of __ physical presence or __ online notarization (Check One)

Type of Identification Produced ___________________

Declaration of Domicile Lee County

DECLARATION OF DOMICILE

To the Clerk of the Circuit Court (County Comptroller of **Lee** County, Florida)
This is my/our declaration of domicile in the State of Florida that
I am/ we are filing this day in accordance and in conformity with
Section 222.17, Florida Statutes.

For Recording Information only:

I/we became a resident on: ______________________

I/we hereby declare that I/we reside in and maintain a place of abode at:

____
(Street and number)

______________________ Florida ______________________
(City and county) (Zip)

Which place of abode I/we recognize and intend to maintain as my permanent home and, if I/we maintain another place or places of abode in some other state or states, I/we hereby declare that my/our above described residence and abode in the State of Florida constitutes my/our predominant and principal home, and I/we intend to continue it permanently as such. I am, at the time of making this declaration, a bona fide resident of the State of Florida residing at:

____
(Street and number)

______________________ Florida ______________________
(City and county) (Zip)

And the place or places where I/we maintain another or other place or places of abode are as follows: (Here list street address, city, county, and state of any other place or places of abode.)

I/we maintain another abode at:	I/we formerly resided at:
______________________ (Street and number)	______________________ (Street and number)
______________________ (City, County, State, and Zip)	______________________ (City, County, State, and Zip)

MUST BE signed in front of a Notary

______________________ Signature	______________________ Signature
______________________ Printed Name	______________________ Printed Name

Sworn before me by means of [ ] physical presence or [ ] audio-video communication technology, this _____day of ____________20_____, by ______________________ who [ ] is personally know to me or [ ] produced ______________________ as identification.

Place Notary Stamp here:

____
(Signature of Notary Public, State of Florida)

____
(Print, type or stamp commissioned name of Notary Public)

Declaration of Domicile Manatee County

DECLARATION OF DOMICILE

To the Clerk of the Circuit Court (County Controller) Manatee County, Florida.

This is my declaration of domicile in the State of Florida, that I am filing this day in accordance and in conformity with Section 222.17, Florida Statutes.

FOR DOMICILIARIES OF THE STATE OF FLORIDA:

I hereby declare that I reside in and maintain a place of abode at ______________________________, (street and number) ______________, ______________, Manatee County, Florida, which place of abode I recognize and (city) (zip code) intend to maintain as my permanent home and, if I maintain another place or places of abode in some other state or states, I hereby declare that my above-described residence and abode in the State of Florida constitutes my predominant and principal home, and I intend to continue it permanently as such. I am, at the time of making this declaration, a bona fide resident of the State of Florida residing at ______________, ______________, ______________, Manatee County, Florida. (street and number) (city) (zip code)
I formerly resided at ______________, ______________ County, ______________ (city) (county) (state)
and the place or places where I maintain another or other place or places of abode are as follows:
(Here list street address, city, county and state of any other place or places of abode)

______________________________ ______________________________
(Print Name) (Print Name)

______________________________ ______________________________
(Signature) (Signature)

State of Florida County of Manatee
Sworn to and subscribed before me by means of ☐physical presence or ☐online notarization this ________ day of ______________, A.D. 20 ______, by ______________________________ who has produced identification in the form of ______________________.

By: ______________________________
Signature and Title of Notarizing or Attesting Official

FOR DOMICILIARIES OF STATE OTHER THAN THE STATE OF FLORIDA:

I hereby declare that my domicile is in the State of ______________ and that I intend to permanently continue and maintain my domicile in such state. At the time of making this declaration I am a bona fide resident of the State of ______________. My place of abode within the State of Florida, if any, is as follows: (Here list street address, city, and county of place of abode in Florida.)

(Person making declaration may also include such other and further facts with reference to any acts done or performed by such person which such person desires or intends not to be construed as evidencing any intention to establish his domicile within the State of Florida)

____
(signature)

State of ______________ County of ______________
Sworn to and subscribed before me by means of ☐physical presence or ☐online notarization this ______ day of ______________, A.D. 20 ______, by ______________________________ who has produced identification in the form of ______________________.

____
Signature and Title of Notarizing or Attesting Official

THIS IS NOT AN APPLICATION FOR HOMESTEAD EXEMPTION.
To apply for Homestead Exemption you must go to the Property Appraiser, 915 4th Ave. W., Bradenton.

Declaration of Domicile Martin County

DECLARATION OF DOMICILE

To the Clerk of the Circuit Court Martin County, Florida.

This is my declaration of domicile in the State of Florida that I am filing this day of , in accordance and in conformity with Section 222.17, Florida Statutes.
FOR DOMICILIARIES OF THE STATE OF FLORIDA:

I hereby declare that I reside in and maintain a place of abode at:

____
(Street and number)

____________________________________ Florida
(City and county)

which place of abode I recognize and intend to maintain as my permanent home and, if I maintain another place or places of abode in some other state or states, I hereby declare that my above-described residence and abode in the State of Florida constitutes my predominant and principal home, and I intend to continue it permanently as such. I am, at the time of making this declaration, a bona fide resident of the State of Florida residing at:

____
(Street and number)

____________________________________ Florida
(City and county)

I formerly resided at:

____
(Street and number)

____
(City and county) (State)

and the place or places where I maintain another or other place or places of abode are as follows:
(Here list street address, city, county and state of any other place or places of abode.)

____

____________________ ____________________
(Print name) (Signature)

Sworn to and subscribed before me this ______ day of __________________, 20____, by
____.

____
Signature of Notary Public/Deputy Clerk, State of Florida

____
Print, type or stamp commissioned name of Notary Public
Personally known_________ or (check one)
Produced Identification____________
Type of Identification Produced:

Declaration of Domicile Miami-Dade County

DECLARATION OF DOMICILE

TO THE STATE OF FLORIDA AND
COUNTY OF MIAMI-DADE:

This is my Declaration of Domicile in the State of Florida that I am filing this day in accordance, and in conformity with Section 222.17, Florida Statutes.

I, ________________________ was formerly a legal resident of ________________________
(Print Name) (City)

________________ and I resided at ________________________, however, I have changed my
(State) (Street Address)

Domicile to and have been a bona fide resident of the State of Florida since the _____ day of ________________, 20_____. I now

reside at ________________________, ________________________.
(Street Address) (City)

Miami-Dade County, Florida, and this statement is to be taken as my declaration of actual legal residence and permanent domicile in this State and County to the exclusion of all others, and I will comply with all requirements of legal residents of Florida.

I understand that as a legal resident of Florida: I must purchase Florida license plates for motor vehicles, if any, owned by me, and/or my spouse; if I vote, I must vote in the precinct of my legal domicile and that my estate will be probated in the Florida Courts.

I was born in the U.S.A.: ☐ Yes ☐ No Place of Birth: ________________________

Naturalized Citizen - Where: ________________ Date: ________________ No. ________________

Lawful Permanent Resident: Date: ________________ No. ________________

____
(Signature)

____
(Print Name)

____
(Mailing Address)

STATE OF FLORIDA
COUNTY OF MIAMI-DADE

Sworn to and subscribed before me this _______ day of ________________________, 20_______,

by ________________________ ☐ personally known to me or ☐ who has produced a ________________________ as identification and did take an oath.

____
Signature of Notary Public, State of Florida

____
Print, Type or Stamp name of notary

You are required to fill-out and notarize the form. When complete, bring or mail original to the County Recorder's Office at 22 NW 1st St., Miami, Florida 33128 with a $10 (money order or cash if coming in person) with a self-addressed stamped envelope.

Penalty for perjury: up to five (5) years in State Prison and $5,000 fine (F.S. 837.02)

Declaration of Domicile Orange County

Warning: Orange County Public Schools no longer requires this form.
ADVERTENCIA: Las escuelas públicas del Condado de Orange ya no requieren este formulario

DECLARATION OF DOMICILE *(Declaración de Domicilio)*
FOR DOMICILIARIES OF THE STATE OF FLORIDA:
(Para residentes en el Estado de la Florida:)

This is my declaration of domicile in the State of Florida that I am filing this day in accordance and in conformity with Section 222.17, Florida Statutes.
(Esta es mi declaración de domicilio en el Estado de la Florida, que estoy registrando en éste día de acuerdo y en conformidad con la Sección 222.17, de los Estatutos de la Florida.)

1. **I hereby declare that I am a bona fide resident of the State of Florida, and reside in and maintain a place of abode at:** *(Por la presente declaro que resido y mantengo mi residencia en:)*

____, Orange County, Florida
Address (Dirección) City and Zip Code *(Ciudad y Codigo Postal)*

which place of abode I recognize and intend to maintain as my permanent home and, if I maintain another place or places of abode in some other state or states, I hereby declare that my above-described residence and abode in the State of Florida constitutes my predominant and principal home, and I intend to continue it permanently as such. *(lugar de residencia el cual reconozco e intento mantener como mi hogar permanente y, de mantener otro lugar[es] como residencia[s] en cualquier otro estado[s], declaro en la presente que mi residencia descrita anteriormente y hogar en el Estado de Florida constituye mi hogar principal y predominante, y mi intención es continuar de esa manera permanentemente.)*

2. **I formerly resided at:** *(Mi residencia anterior era:)*

____,
Address *(Dirección)* City, County, State and Zip Code *(Ciudad, Condado, Estado y Codigo Postal)*

3. **The place or places where I maintain another or other place or places of abode are as follows:** (Indicate street address, city, county, and state of any other place or places of abode.) *(y el lugar[es] donde mantengo otra[s] residencias son los siguientes): (Indique aquí las calles, ciudades, condados y estados de cualquier otro lugar[es] de residenci [s].)*

____,
Address *(Dirección)* City, County, State and Zip Code *(Ciudad, Condado, Estado y Codigo Postal)*

____
Signature *(Firma)*

____
Printed Name *(Nombre en letra de molde)*

Sworn to and subscribed before me this *(Jurado y suscrito ante mi hoy)* ________ of __________, 20____.
Day Month Year
Phil Diamond, COUNTY COMPTROLLER, ORANGE COUNTY *(CONTRALOR del CONDADO ORANGE)*

By______________________________
DEPUTY COMPTROLLER *(DIPUTADO del CONTRALOR)*

OR (O)

State of _______________
County of _______________
Sworn to (or affirmed) and subscribed before me by means of [ ] physical presence or [ ] online notarization,this ______ ______ day of __________________, ________ by ______________________
who is _______ personally known to me
OR produced ______________________________ as identification.

Notary Signature and Seal______________________________

Revised 1/1/2020

Declaration of Domicile Osceola County

DECLARATION OF DOMICILE *(Declaración de Domicilio)*
FOR DOMICILIARIES OF THE STATE OF FLORIDA:
(Para residentes en el Estado de la Florida:)

This is my declaration of domicile in the State of Florida that I am filing this day in accordance and in conformity with Section 222.17, Florida Statutes.
(Esta es mi declaración de domicilio en el Estado de la Florida, que estoy registrando en éste día de acuerdo y en conformidad con la Sección 222.17, de los Estatutos de la Florida.)

1. **I hereby declare that I am a bona fide resident of the State of Florida, and reside in and maintain a place of abode at:** *(Por la presente declaro que resido y mantengo mi residencia en:)*

____, Osceola County, Florida
Address (Dirección) City and Zip Code *(Ciudad y Codigo Postal)*

which place of abode I recognize and intend to maintain as my permanent home and, if I maintain another place or places of abode in some other state or states, I hereby declare that my above-described residence and abode in the State of Florida constitutes my predominant and principal home, and I intend to continue it permanently as such. *(lugar de residencia el cual reconozco e intento mantener como mi hogar permanente y, de mantener otro lugar[es] como residencia[s] en cualquier otro estado[s], declaro en la presente que mi residencia descrita anteriormente y hogar en el Estado de Florida constituye mi hogar principal y predominante, y mi intención es continuar de esa manera permanentemente.)*

2. **I formerly resided at:** *(Mi residencia anterior era:)*

____,
Address (Dirección) City, County, State and Zip Code *(Ciudad, Condado, Estado y Codigo Postal)*

3. **The place or places where I maintain another or other place or places of abode are as follows:** (Indicate street address, city, county, and state of any other place or places of abode.) *(y el lugar[es] donde mantengo otra[s] residencias son los siguientes): (Indique aquí las calles, ciudades, condados y estados de cualquier otro lugar[es] de residenci [s].)*

____,
Address *(Dirección)* City, County, State and Zip Code *(Ciudad, Condado, Estado y Codigo Postal)*

____
Signature *(Firma)*

____
Printed Name *(Nombre en letra de molde)*

State of __________
County of ____________

Sworn to (or affirmed) and subscribed before me by means of [ ] physical presence or [ ] online notarization,
this _____ day of ______________________, ________ by ______________________________

who is_______ personally known to me

OR produced______________________________as identification.

Notary Signature and Seal ______________________________

Revised 6/24/2021

Declaration of Domicile Palm Beach County

DECLARATION OF DOMICILE

For Domiciliaries of the State of Florida:

To the Clerk of the Circuit Court (County Comptroller) of Palm Beach County, Florida.

This is my declaration of domicile in the State of Florida that I am filing this day in accordance and in conformity with Section 222.17, Florida Statutes.

I ______________________________ hereby declare that I reside in and maintain a place of abode at:

____
(street and number)

______________________________ , Florida
(city and county)

which place of abode I recognize and intend to maintain as my permanent home and, if I maintain another place or places of abode in some other state or states, I hereby declare that my above-described residence and abode in the State of Florida constitutes my predominant and principal home, and I intend to continue it permanently as such. I am, at the time of making this declaration, a bona fide resident of the State of Florida residing at:

____
(street and number)

______________________________ , Florida
(city and county)

I formerly resided at:

____
(street and number)

____
(city, county and state)

and the place or places where I maintain another or other place or places of abode are as follows: (Here list street address, city, county, and state of any other place or places of abode.)

____
(Signature)

Sworn to (or affirmed) and subscribed before me by means of ◯ physical presence or ◯ online notarization, this ____ day of __________________, ______ by: ______________________________ personally known to me, or who produced ____________________ as identification.

____
(Signature of Notary Public, State of Florida)

____
(Print, type or stamp commissioned name of Notary Public)

121416 **(See reverse side for Domiciliaries of States Other than the State of Florida)**

Declaration of Domicile Pinellis County

DECLARATION OF DOMICILE

To the Clerk of the Circuit Court County Comptroller of ______________ County, Florida.

This is my declaration of domicile in the State of Florida that I am filing this day in accordance and in conformity with Section 222.17, Florida Statutes.

FOR DOMICILIARIES OF THE STATE OF FLORIDA:

I ________________________ hereby declare that I reside in and maintain a place of abode at:

____
(street and number)

______________________________________ , Florida
(city and county)

which place of abode I recognize and intend to maintain as my permanent home and, if I maintain another place or places of abode in some other state or states, I hereby declare that my above-described residence and abode in the State of Florida constitutes my predominant and principal home, and I intend to continue it permanently as such. I am, at the time of making this declaration, a bona fide resident of the State of Florida residing at:

____
(street and number)

______________________________________ , Florida
(city and county)

I formerly resided at:

____
(street and number)

______________________________________ , Florida
(city and county)

and the place or places where I maintain another or other place or places of abode are as follows: (Here list street address, city, county, and state of any other place or places of abode.)

____
(Signature)

Sworn to and subscribed before me this ____ of ___________________, ______.

____

(Signature of Notary Public, State of Florida)

____

(Print, type or stamp commissioned name of Notary Public)

Personally Known ______ or Produced Identification ______

(Check One)

Type of Identification Produced: ____________________

(See reverse side for Domiciliaries of States Other than the State of Florida)

FOR DOMICILIARIES OF STATES OTHER THAN THE STATE OF FLORIDA:

I ______________________ hereby declare that my domicile is in the State of __________ and that I intend to permanently continue and maintain my domicile in such state. At the time of making this declaration I am a bona fide resident of the State of __________. My place of abode within the State of Florida, if any, is as follows: (Here list street address, city, and county of place of abode in Florida.)

(Person making declaration may also include such other and further facts with reference to any acts done or performed by such person which such person desires or intends not to be construed as evidencing any intention to establish his/her domicile within the State of Florida.)

____

(Signature)

Sworn to and subscribed before me this________ of____________________, ______.

____

(Signature of Notary Public, State of Florida)

____

(Print, type or stamp commissioned name of Notary Public)

Personally Known _____ or Produced Identification _____
(Check One)

Type of Identification Produced: ____________________

Declaration of Domicile St. Lucie County

MICHELLE R. MILLER
CLERK & COMPTROLLER
ST. LUCIE COUNTY, FLORIDA

RECORDING DEPARTMENT
201 S. Indian River Drive, 4th floor, Fort Pierce, FL 34950
772-462-6928

DECLARATION OF DOMICILE

To the Clerk & Comptroller of St. Lucie County, Florida.

This is my declaration of domicile in the State of Florida that I am filing this day in accordance and in conformity with Section 222.17, Florida Statutes.

FOR DOMICILIARIES OF THE STATE OF FLORIDA

GENERAL INFORMATION / PLEASE PRINT CLEARLY		
First Name	Middle Name	Last Name
Permanent Street Address		
Permanent City	State Florida	Zip

I hereby declare that I reside in and maintain a place of abode at the above address, which I recognize and intend to maintain as my permanent home and, if I maintain another place or places of abode in some other state or states, I hereby declare that my above-described residence and abode in the State of Florida constitutes my predominant and principal home, and I intend to continue it permanently as such. I am, at the time of making this declaration, a bona fide resident of the State of Florida residing at:

Current Street Address		
Current City	State Florida	Zip

I formerly resided at the below address and the place or places where I maintain another or other places of abode are as follows: (Here list street address, city, county, and state of any other place or places of abode.)

Former Street Address		
Former City	Former State	Former Zip

Signature ____________________

Sworn to and subscribed before me this _____ (day) of _____ (month), 20 ____

MICHELLE R. MILLER
CLERK & COMPTROLLER
ST. LUCIE COUNTY, FLORIDA

By: ____________________
Deputy Clerk

(Seal)

____
(Signature of Notary Public, State of Florida)

____
(Print, type, or stamp commissioned name of Notary Public)

___ Personally Known or ___ Produced Identification
(Check one)

Type of Identification Produced: ________________

INDEX

NOTES

Made in the USA
Monee, IL
05 November 2026

67387505R00074